RETURNING THE ELEPHANT
INTO THE CITY

RETURNING THE ELEPHANT INTO THE CITY

The Unfinished Contract with Ghana

Charles K. Addo

RETURNING THE ELEPHANT INTO THE CITY
THE UNFINISHED CONTRACT WITH GHANA

iUniverse books may be ordered through booksellers or by contacting:

iUniverse
1663 Liberty Drive
Bloomington, IN 47403
www.iuniverse.com
1-800-Authors (1-800-288-4677)

ISBN: 978-1-4917-6345-2 (sc)
ISBN: 978-1-4917-6346-9 (e)

Print information available on the last page.

iUniverse rev. date: 03/23/2015

TABLE OF CONTENTS

PREFACE

"When falls on man the anger of the gods, first from his mind they banish understanding."

-LYCURGUS

Ghana faces daunting challenges from the socio-economic front. These challenges run the whole gamut, from corruption to education to health care to unemployment to cultural issues, to name only a few major ones. These myriad of socio-economic challenges that stare Ghana in the face require solutions from experienced and committed leadership; not uncommitted, inexperienced, trial-and-error kind of leadership. People who understand that the true worth of an individual is not how much material wealth one can accumulate, though it's important, but those who know the true meaning of giving back to the world and care very deeply about the world and posterity. Experienced people, generally, tend to exhibit more of such traits.

The contract with Ghana is an implied adherence and commitment to certain systematic public policies that aims at quickening the pace of Ghana's socio-economic development for which a political party is elected into office to prosecute. It involves fiscal discipline, probity, and accountability in governance to permit resources to be channeled to where they are most needed, such as education, health, roads, water, energy, and agricultural sectors. This contract has seen neglect, stagnation, and non-performance for over six years under the NDC administration. It is imperative now that the contract be revived and performed by the NPP for the true well-being of all Ghanaians. The two main vehicles of this contract for achieving rapid socio-economic development are education for the citizenry and corruption-free leadership. Lack of education and enlightenment breed ignorance and naïve citizens, who are unable to scrutinize effectively developmental policies and are easily preyed upon by some politicians and some religious leaders who swindle them out of their rights. Corruption is evidenced by weak and ineffective social institutions that allow misdirection of public resources for socio-economic development, and accrue only to the benefits of private and few individual interests.

For the NDC, a socialist party that do not believe in property ownership, yet clandestinely recognizes that property ownership is a natural human desire only after winning power, the risk of embezzlement from state coffers to fund ownership of property can be logically expected. That is why we see unprecedented acts of corruption and mismanagement of state assets under the NDC government. That is why the property-owning NPP is truly the party of the masses. The property-owning party does not need to first greedily appropriate for itself state resources before giving back to the people. That is why the elephant party is truly, the party of choice for most ordinary people. After all, politics and political parties, at best, involve dealing with two necessary evils in the human condition: haves and have-nots. The haves, unlike the have-nots, already have their mouths full and are relatively disinclined to gluttony or over eating. That is why it would be most rewarding to vote massively for the haves than the have-nots; for their mouths are already full and there is not enough room to hold additional bites from the national cake. That means they leave the national cake with everyone having a share, and are better positioned to deliver opportunities and prosperity to the masses.

Not long ago, the leadership of the NDC government was reported to have stated before a gathering in Germany that "however bad a government is, it contributes to moving the nation forward and other people take over and continue."[1] Obviously, this was an implicit admission that the NDC government was underperforming, and that however bad its performance, it is a necessary step to idle the engine of the nation's socio-economic development, until a better administration takes over and steer it in the right direction. It was, unmistakably, an admission of failure; and a hallmark of desperation. A bad government and poor leadership rather destroy a nation. This is a self-evident fact. It is quite absurd that the NDC leadership cannot understand the direct relationship that exists between good governance and good macroeconomic performance; and that there

---

[1] "Even bad gov'ts contribute to nation building — Mahama," (2015).

is no room, whatsoever, for a bad government in the forward movement to socio-economic development.

The issues of the 2016 election, is not about the role of bad governance in nation building. The issues of the 2016 election has everything to do with the scandalous level of unemployment of millions of our young people, the apparent tacit and pervasive official corruption which has impoverished Ghanaians, and the lack of concern of the NDC government; as exemplified by its dance to the tune of Lumba's famous release, "Yentie Obiara," meaning "we won't listen to the cry of anybody" in the country irrespective of the level of maladministration. The issue of the 2016 election is about the role of good leadership in nation building; about "a leadership that can manage the economy with discipline, vision and innovation."[2]

This book is a brief socio-economic analysis and lesson for the elephant party, the NPP, as to why it was "chased into the bush" in 2008 in Ghana, and to serve as a guide and expectations for its "return into the city" in 2016. It is an attempt to put together facts that already exist in the public domain in one way or the other for the voters. The aim is to enable voters, after reading this book, to see a snapshot of events in governance in Ghana in the last few years, and make them better decision makers in the 2016 elections. Election 2016 is obviously not going to be an easy one, but the odds are very much tilted in favor of the elephant party. One reason is the Supreme Court petition in 2012, which was essentially a trial of the temperament, character, and disposition of the NPP presidential candidate and flagbearer, Nana Akufo-Addo. The odds are also very much in favor of the NPP due to the fact that the NDC, the self-proclaimed socialist party, has become so deeply embroiled in corruption and financial malfeasance that it has really lost the goodwill of a significant number of the voters. For example, the Woyome Scandal, GYEEDA, SADA, $3 Million Airlift to Brazil. It is precisely because of these acts of unprecedented corruption that the NDC is most determined to put up its fiercest fight to retain power—fear of the application of the law of causing financial loss to the state.

---

[2]   "Management of economy requires discipline — Akufo-Addo," (2015).

This book also predicts a likely scenario just prior to the NPP capturing power in the 2016 elections. It is especially intended to ensure that peace prevails in election 2016. This is not to say that corruption should ever be connived and condoned in public officialdom. For that will be sending a wrong signal and a very dangerous precedence for our socio-economic development. Crime is crime and the law must always take its course. An avowed purpose of this book is to help avoid election violence. That when "push should come to a shove," contending parties and stakeholders will be guided by the awareness that there is room for negotiation to de-escalate any tension and avoid violence in the country at all cost. After all, nobody is a winner when we sit on the fence and watch Decision 2016 engulfed in flames.

It is my fervent hope that present and future Ghanaian leaders will begin to see this book as a huge starting point and a departure from the politics of selfishness and money grabbing in public service, and to achieve the needed "elevation" to see the sad situation of Ghana, some 58 years after attaining political independence, and say, "What have we really achieved after all these years of agitation and attaining political independence?" Indeed, it is very much still an "unfinished agenda" for Ghanaians, until we yield to patriotism. And this book casts a broader spotlight on patriotism that the NDC is amply lacking. Finally, this book is likely to stir up voters' intense excitement for decision 2016 that hopefully, will begin and contribute to a serious national conversation about the bad state of the economy, a result of the handiwork of the NDC administration. This will sharpen voters' awareness and make them better positioned to see the best party to vote for, which I believe given the NDC's dismal performance, will not find favor in the eyes of the voting public.

Dr. Charles K. Addo

Ghana

ACKNOWLEDGMENTS

Machiavelli noted some 500 years ago that neutrality falls prey to the winner, as he is considered a dubious friend; and to the loser not a friend, as he did not come to its defense. Writing this book immersed me in the interstices of religion, patriotism, and the 2016 elections. I asked myself on several occasions: "Why do you want to go out publicly and give certain information away?" There were times that I quailed before the arduous task of those that it would make and those that it would break. But the truth will ever remain the truth. I found solace within the deepest recesses of my conscience. I want to express my particular gratitude to those who gave me useful suggestions and encouragement. I want to thank Mr. Paul Osei Brafi for his assistance in helping me expand my vision and sharpen my prose.

CHAPTER ONE

Understanding the Socio-Economic background of Ghana

The socio-economic performance of Sub-Sahara Africa (SSA), including Ghana, is far less than desirable. SSA countries have huge gaps in sectors that include health, water, energy, roads, education, and agriculture. At the same time, governments in these regions are constrained by financial, institutional, and human capital resources that they urgently require so that they might be able to close these gaps or, at least, reduce these shortfalls. Apart from making residents of SSA countries finding themselves under abject poverty, these problems also chip away the respect and dignity of people who come from these regions. It is, therefore, absolutely necessary for these governments to manage with prudence the limited resources that they have in order to fulfill the aspirations of its present citizens and future generations. Some have attempted to assign the root causes of these poor socio-economic development to culture and colonial legacy; others have attributed the causes to corrupt practices and institutions; and yet others to educational systems that do not effectively respond to our economic developmental needs, making the education sector particularly a punching bag for reform every now and then by the strong arm of political expediency. Let us see briefly how each of those causes adversely impact on the economic development of Ghana.

Culture and Colonial Legacy

Beginning in the 1960s, when the sweeping wind of political independence started blowing cross SSA, virtually all geographic areas of the world have experienced some improvements in their incomes relative to the Organization for Economic Co-operation and Development (OECD), or at

1

least remained unchanged, except for SSA, including Ghana, which has seen dramatic economic underperformance. The per capita incomes in the OECD, by 2005, were $36,780 as compared with the SSA of $746.[3] Established in 1961, the OECD is an international economic organization that comprise of 34 countries, with the objective of stimulating economic progress and world trade, commitment to democracy, and adherence to the market economy. It is a forum of countries that supply a platform to compare policy experiences, seek solutions to common problems, identify good practices, and coordinate policies of its member countries.[4]

Bringing it closer home, the trend in the socio-economic condition of Ghana appears to mirror closely that of SSA states, making some people wondering what is wrong with SSA states, and some even growing so pessimistic as to capitulate to the suggestion of "hopelessness." For example, at the first Alhaji Aliu Mahama Lectures delivered on 13th November 2013, the NPP running mate of Nana Akufo-Addo, Dr. Mahamudu Bawumia, noted a very disturbing trend regarding Ghana's socio-economic development. At the time of Ghana's independence in 1957, the country's foreign exchange reserves was $2.275 billion in today's money value with zero external or domestic debt for a population of only 6.5 million people. This contrasted with gross international reserves of $2.03 billion with a debt stock of $8 billion for a population of about 23 million in 2008. Under this macroeconomic scenario in 1957, by 1984 Ghana had piled up external debt of 27% of Gross Domestic Product (GDP), which increased dramatically in 1994 to 103% of GDP, and even further up to 182% of GDP by 2000, with an economic growth rate that stood at 3.7%. The country was now experiencing severe difficulty servicing its debt obligations. This was the macro-economic picture when the NPP administration took over in 2000. At 2008, after eight years of the NPP governance, the external debt to GDP ratio had dramatically been brought down from 182% to 32%, with an economic growth rate of 8.4% that relied solely on traditional exports, without the benefit of a newly-found oil production. Ghana was poised to take its place among lower middle income economies, from a low income Highly Indebted

---

3   UNDP, Human Development Report (2001); World Bank, World Development Report (2006).
4   Wikipedia, "Organisation for Economic Co-operation and Development." (2015).

Poor Country (HIPC) economy. This also was the state of the national economy at the time the NDC administration assumed governance in 2008 under Atta-Mills. By 2011, with the benefit of oil revenue, the economy expanded by some 15% and in 2012 the real GDP growth including the benefit of oil revenue was 7.9%. At the end of 2012, Ghana's budget deficit stood at GH¢8.7 billion, representing 12.0% of GDP. This amount was the highest budget deficit ever recorded in the history of Ghana, from the governments of Nkrumah through Acheampong, Rawlings, and Kufuor. The primary reason for this huge budget deficit was that government spending in 2012 increased very dramatically by over 100% to 34.5% of GDP compared to government revenue of 16.1% of GDP. This was a result of the NDC government, under John Mahama, jettisoning all fiscal discipline overboard, in its desire to win the 2012 elections. This landed Ghana in a total public debt that increased from GH¢ 9.5 billion in 2008 to GH¢43.9 billion as at August 2013, an increase of 357% in less than a period of 5 years.[5]

It has been placed on record by certain observers[6] through their studies that the gravitation towards non-competitive socio-economic behavior by SSA countries can be placed squarely at the doorstep of culture and the vestige of colonial legacy. However, there is a lack of general consensus regarding the true impact of those factors on the socio-economic development of countries south of the Sahara, with studies depicting varied results.[7]

Prominent international organizations, such as the International Monetary Fund, the World Bank, and the United Nations Development Program have suggested that this absence of socio-economic progression by SSA nations is a direct result of the lack of competitiveness, inadequate entrepreneurial spirit, and non-embracing of the free market system. To remedy such economically retrogressive condition calls for the adoption of a wide range of policies, that can reduce restrictions decreed by culture, social, and political behaviors.[8] It is in line with this thinking

---

[5]   "NDC govt practising 'Akonfem socialism' – Bawumia," (2013).
[6]   Glaeser, La Porta, Lopez-de-Silanes, & Schleifer, (2004).
[7]   Uy, (2009).
[8]   Cammack, (2006).

that some observers[9] suggest a connection between culture and economic development. Carrying on with the work of one seminal researcher,[10] inquiries have been expanding that suggest that historical influences do have effect on SSA countries present condition of socio-economic retrogression.[11]

The concept of culture is not amenable to precise definition, and requires different operational constructs that measure each of its subparts. According to Hodgetts and Luthans,[12] the Dutch researcher, Hofstede, identified four subparts of culture, namely:

1. Power distance or the extent to which less powerful group members of organizations accept that power is not equally distributed among members of society;
2. Uncertainty avoidance or the extent to which people feel threatened by ambiguous situations, and have established beliefs and institutions that they perceive keep them safe;
3. Individualism or the tendency for people to look after themselves and their immediate family only;
4. Collectivism or the tendency of people to associate in groups or collectives and to seek a common interest or look after each other in exchange for loyalty.

Because of the lack of precise definition of culture, researchers tend to utilize either a single or a set of dimensional variables such as, power distance culture of Ghanaians or power distance and collectivism culture of Ghanaians respectively.[13] Perhaps, what is even more peculiar about culture is the general absence of consensus among researchers as to the superiority of any one culture or a widely accepted culture. This may be because every culture appears to possess some element of superiority over another in certain respects, thus making the definition of culture also non-holistic. Therefore, to measure culture as a whole appears to be

---

9   Platteau, (2009); Glaeser, La Porta, Lopez-de-Silanes, & Schleifer, (2004); Ichino & Maggi, (1999).
10   North, (1981).
11   Hall, & Jones, (1999); Acemoglu, Simon, & Robinson, (2001).
12   Hodgetts & Luthans, (1994).
13   Uy, (2009).

an unrealistic undertaking. Given the connection that appears to exist between culture and socio-economic development, it raises the question of what is the essence of culture that makes it impact significantly on socio-economic development, and to determine the destiny of countless number of people in SSA countries? This question may be answered by discussing some major concepts of culture.

Tischler attempted to define culture as "all that human beings learn to do, to use, to produce, to know, and to believe as they grow to maturity and live out their lives in the social groups to which they belong."[14] Another study[15] also attempted to deepen the meaning of culture from the perspective of three planes, being, individual, organizational, and national. Viewed from (a) individual standpoint, culture is how people interact and express their values; (b) organizational standpoint, it is how people within an organization interact and express attitudes; and (c) national standpoint, it is how attitudes are expressed in a particular country or geographical region. The study further charted a definition for culture by noting that every culture exhibits its own way for solving a specific problem that reveals itself as dilemmas. Yet another study[16] elucidated on the concept of culture by noting that it is evaluated based on individual values and beliefs, such as (a) trust and respect for others and (b) confidence in individual self-determination. This study further noted that historically, two major variables that are employed as tools to isolate the exogenous variation in culture are the literacy rate and political institutions.

To shed more light on the mechanics of the above studies, probably the attitude exhibited by two leaders from different geographical regions reveals how culture is expressed at the national level. When US President Barack Obama was faced with a shooting crisis involving civilians by a US soldier in Afghanistan, he urged his officials by stating that he "supported" them in resolving the issue[17.] Thus Mr. Obama was, in effect, expressing trust, respect for his officials, and confidence in the officials' self-determination. Here, there is an implied assumption that

---

[14] Tischler, (1993).
[15] Trompenaars, (1994).
[16] Tabellini, (2010).
[17] "Obama: US soldier's reported shooting rampage," (2012).

the investigative authorities did not require any outside prompting to do its work. The attitude was different when Ghana's ex-President Prof. Atta-Mills was confronted with a case of a party financier who duped the state of public funds by "directing" authorities to initiate investigations.[18] Here, there is the absence of trust, respect for others, and lack of confidence in individual self-determination or institutional self-determination. There exists an implied assumption of not recognizing and respecting the ability of the institution created precisely to deal with such issues, and that the institution lacked the initiative to conduct investigations unless it received external prompting or direction before performing its function.

These two attitudes exhibited by the two leaders at national levels of culture are symptoms of the leaders, and constitute a part of the respective national and media psyche of the two countries. It has happened many times and keeps happening in the Ghanaian culture and halls of governance where, such orders and directions from above, only point to weak institutions.

It is worthy of note that one study[19] observed a link between economic development and individualism. This subpart of culture, individualism, was scored high by Hofstede,[20] among developed economies. This subpart of culture has the attribute of a nuclear family system or a group's desire to look after themselves and immediate family members. Its converse, collectivism, also scored high among least developed economies that are characterized by the extended family systems or the attribute of a group to look after its members. Thus, the relationship that is found between poverty and the extended family system in Ghana may have its ancestry from this dimension of culture or collectivism. This is because not only does it chip away the initiative and self-reliance spirit of individual members within the group, but also it renders them complacent. This, by no means, is an endorsement of any anti-collective practices. Rather, it is to point out that there must be some amount of cultural paradigm shift in this area to permit Ghana to progress socio-economically. After all, the complacency that comes with a group member dwelling in the cozy sense

---

[18] "President J.E.A. Mills orders EOCO to investigate," (2011).

[19] Weber, (1970).

[20] Hofstede, (1991).

of collective protection and its social safety net can have an adverse way of affecting, for example, one's work ethics, and hence national productivity.

Researchers[21] have also documented that although institutions may be created alike, they may work differently in different environments, giving a hint that informal institutions such as culture do influence the operation of institutions. For example, this study noted that the judicial system in the northern and southern Italy, even though they are all within the same country, functioned differently to some degree, with court judges in the north ruling on civil cases faster than those located in the southern regions. Another study[22] buttressed such regional differences in the way hospitals, schools, and public administrations functioned. Such ethnic or regional differentiations may generate unequal development of modern citizenship, and result in endogenous socio-economic underdevelopment; persistence of informal rules and social norms that perpetuate legal dualism, which works against the credibility of modern statutory laws that are designed to foster socio-economic development.[23] Similarly, in Ghana, social customs and norms, for example prolonged time and efforts devoted to funeral activities may hinder differentiation of economic and social life that lead to a reduction in both individual and aggregate capital formation, resulting in reduced performance of business enterprises. Thus, one may infer that economic development has partial roots in culture.

Colonial legacy is an umbrella term used to describe the political structure, culture, and general polity bequeathed to the elite indigenous ruling class of the new independent states as the colonial governments left those states. For Ghana, this legacy continues to affect the political and socio-economic life, some 58 years after political independence. It was a form of administration that was characterized by oppressive mechanism, having no freewill, consent, or purpose.[24] It, hardly, had any semblance to the modern democratic principles that the developed economies are now requiring from Ghana, using prominent international financial institutions, such as the World Bank and the IMF, to administer

---

21   Glaeser, La Porta, Lopez-de-Silanes, & Schleifer, (2004).
22   Ichino, & Giovanni, (1999).
23   Platteau, (2009); Glaeser, La Porta, Lopez-de-Silanes, & Schleifer, (2004); Ichino & Maggi, (1999).
24   Alemazung, (2010).

socio-economic structural adjustment programs as cure for Ghana's socio-economic ailments. Some studies have shown connections between colonial legacies and postcolonial socio-economic development of countries of SSA, including Ghana. For example, one study[25] has suggested that the poor economic development of Ghana may be a direct result of the extraction and relocation of human resource to the now economically developed countries to meet their labor demand, the rippling effect of which continues to be felt. This observation is supported by one other study[26] that documented that prolonged exploitation under colonial rule has wreaked considerable havoc on the economic development of countries in the SSA. Lange,[27] noted that both direct and indirect rule by the colonial governments were not favorable to the socio-economic development of SSA countries.

As one researcher[28] observed, one negative effect of the colonial activities was the purposeful emphasis on ethnic differences, when none really did exist, as a way of promoting the agenda of divide-and-rule strategy to sabotage a unified front against colonial rule. Thus by this behavior, tribalism was invented, which several years later, would be used by presidential candidates to canvass for electoral votes.[29] From the literature discussion above, one can formulate intuitive and empirical conclusion that both culture and colonial legacy may explain, in part, the poor condition of Ghana's socio-economic development. But this condition cannot entirely be blamed on the colonial government, as we shall be learning shortly under the next section. In fact, the Ghanaian proverb that "one can only be bitten by an insect that is lodged inside one's own clothes" has a very strong significance here. A major blame for Ghana's present poor socio-economic performance can be placed squarely at the doorstep of some of Ghana's own leaders. Ghana has leadership problem, with some of its own current leaders consciously under-developing Ghana through corruption and the pursuit of their own parochial interests. Those few selfish leaders are able to perpetuate corruption practices on the people

---

[25]   Nunn, (2007).

[26]   Bertocchi & Canova, (2002).

[27]   Lange, (2004).

[28]   Shillington, (1989).

[29]   "Mahama's dangerous ethnic tirades," (2012); "Nana invades Mills' backyard," (2011).

because they now have power and use of state apparatus to do so, taking unprecedented advantage of the ignorance of significant number of less formally educated people who cannot adequately scrutinize government development policies. That is why the NPP, believing in fiscal discipline, made the free SHS education a cornerstone of its 2012 campaign; a cornerstone that the NDC rejected as unsustainable because of Ghana's limited resources. Now, this same NDC is turning around to support, and even trying to plagiarize and arrogate to itself the free SHS education concept; a concept that was originated and long advocated by the NPP. For example, Dr. Bawumia observed that under the NDC administration in the latter part of 2012, fiscal indiscipline due to the elections resulted in Ghana recording unprecedented budget deficit of GH¢8.7 billion, representing 12% of GDP using the rebased GDP numbers. This amount would have been sufficient in financing free SHS education for seven years.[30]

Corrupt Practices and Institutions

Ghana is presently laden with corruption that impedes socio-economic development. This condition might have had its origins from the activities of the colonial relationships. As some researchers[31] observed at the time of the European interaction in West Africa, there were no ethnic divisions. The setting up of a privileged ruling class from among the indigenous group, as part of a strategy to control the indigenous by the colonialists, resulted in opposing groups of two native Ghanaians: privileged ruling group and an unprivileged ruled group. In carrying out their political mandate of exploitation and transferring resources belonging to all Ghanaian indigenous by the indigenous ruling group to the colonialists and helping themselves in the process, the ruled group naturally grew distrustful of the ruling group.

This, somehow, served as the progeny and institutionalization of corruption in the economy of Ghana, which continues today. As the colonial government withdrew and political independence was ushered in, political power and control of government became fully concentrated

---

[30]   "NDC govt practising 'Akonfem socialism' – Bawumia," (2013).
[31]   Mizuno & Okazawa, (2009).

in the hands of the ruling group. At this point, the seeds of distrust on the part of the ruled group and corruption on the part of the ruling group had been sown. As Tabellini[32] observed, a significant subpart of culture is that of trust and respect for others. Distrust, inevitably, whittles away the spirit of commitment, patriotism and ultimately productivity among a social group, depleting confidence in individual self-determination, which can possibly explain Ghana's lackluster socio-economic performance. After all, confidence in individual self-determination is a major constituent of culture. It is also a major entrepreneurial spirit that characterizes entrepreneurs and people who seek to utilize economic opportunities that ultimately lead to general economic development.[33]

The period after independence revealed that political independence did not imply a socio-economic independence as well. Soon it became clear that Ghana's economic, political and cultural systems continued to experience a new form of exploitation called neo-colonialism,[34] as Ghana's economic system succumbed to policies that were formulated by international financial organizations, whose interests were in synchronization with those of the former colonial administrators.[35] This implied that prescribed economic and political policies largely tended to promote the neo-colonialists' interests over that of Ghanaians. This new form of colonization is doing very well because Ghana's socio-economic system has been rendered quite dependent on that of the neo-colonialists.[36]

Thus, one would have expected that under such dismal socio-economic scenario, when our collective interest as a nation is at stake, our present crop of leaders would be guided by this historical experience and show some serious commitment to the socio-economic development of Ghana for the benefit of present and future generations. Instead, what we see are some people in leadership positions, having the avowed aim of enriching themselves at the expense of the state, with one even going to the extent of promising to amass a personal fortune of US$1 million before quitting

---

[32]   Tabellini, (2010).

[33]   Ibid.

[34]   Mwaura, (2005).

[35]   Nkrumah, (1975).

[36]   Odetoyinbo, (1994); Mwaura, (2005).

politics.[37] This is the song and story of why the NPP needs to be returned to power to gather together, once again, the fortunes and resources of Ghana, and to jealously guard and plan against its mismanagement by the NDC government in future for the good of all Ghanaians.

Nonresponsive Educational System to Economic Developmental Needs

Some studies[38] have noted that Ghana has had numerous education reforms and reviews of existing education systems. Those reforms have been necessitated because of the real or perceived reason that the post-independent educational system has not succeeded in emancipating the country from economic under-development. Another reason often cited by the educational authorities for reforming the educational system appears to be politically motivated. For example, the NDC government announced its intention to revert the then four years of Senior High School (SHS) education to three years in 2009.[39] One of the reasons cited by the government for the poor performance in some SHS was not the duration of schooling, but rather improvement on educational standards to strengthen the basic foundation, Junior High Schools (JHS), with qualified teachers and infrastructure. However, those who were in favor of the four-year duration argued that maintaining the duration at four years would help arrest the trend whereby, a high number of students were left idling in the house because they could not meet tertiary institutions' admission requirements due to poor performance, a result of inadequate time to finish the required syllabus.

The problem with the NDC government is that it has a tendency to indulge in diversionary tactics or costly propaganda, which does not really help the country, whenever any situation that poses a dilemma arises. A case in point is the government's recent establishment of a Power Ministry to deal with the "dumsor dumsor" or the recurrent electricity load shedding problem in the country. How is this new ministry going to solve the load shedding problem? It is only going to increase the cost of governance and

---

[37] "The Ethics Of 'Vickileaks'", (2013).
[38] Tonah, (2006); Sedgwick, (2000).
[39] Tettey-Enyo, (2009).

11

the taxpayer's burden. It is a basic knowledge in economics that the size of government increases the cost of government.[40] An information conveyed to the public by the minister of the new ministry, Dr. Kwabena Donkor, was that indebtedness to the tune of about GH¢500 million, with a significant portion of it owed by the same government, to the Electricity Company of Ghana (ECG), was a major factor in the load shedding problem.[41]

Under normal circumstances, if a state institution such as ECG, is facing cash flow problems to maintain its equipments and deliver on its mandate because of its inability to collect its debts, does it warrant the creation of a whole new ministry? The appropriate approach is for ECG to review its debt collection policy, and to use existing institutions to seal off revenue leakages by arresting and prosecuting any theft of its services? It only demonstrates lack of innovation by the NDC government in moving Ghana forward. That is why now is the time to show the NDC government the exit to the opposition chamber, and roll in the experienced, innovative, and problem-solver NPP government. After all, the president himself, Mr. John Mahama, agrees that "however bad a government is, it contributes to moving the nation forward and other people take over and continue." [42] That is why the time is now to return the elephant into the city to complete the unfinished contract with Ghana. The unfinished job of fine-tuning Ghana through much better social interventions such as free SHS education program, and sealing off leakages of public funds that we so much need for the socio-economic development but losing them to private pockets.

Reforms in education in Ghana appear not to have any well-charted planning. This is probably a reason why we continue to face challenges that have been leading to incessant calls for reform, every now and then.[43] Probably, the most dramatic reform was the phasing out the GCE O-Level and A-Level system, which was patterned after the British educational model. There was nothing that was really wrong with the GCE system, except the desire for change under revolutionary and post-revolutionary zeal, just for the sake of change. The GCE was an effective pre-tertiary education filtration system that assured academic quality. It also served as

---

[40]   Kunateh, (2013).
[41]   "ECG on the brink of collapse– Power Minister," (2015).
[42]   "Even bad gov'ts contribute to nation building — Mahama," (2015).
[43]   Tonah, (2006).

a necessary latent function by reducing the speed with which young adults' enter the labor market, and thereby bringing down the unemployment rate.[44]

One study[45] has noted that contemporary graduates of our SHS system show poor academic skills, with weak command of essential skills that are required of an SHS graduate. Gayton and Bignold[46] observed that it is inappropriate to undertake educational reform that transposes one entire system over another, but rather to use some of the positive aspects inherent in the other to effect improvement to one's educational system. As a result of this, the educational foundation of Ghana is experiencing erosion by a rising tide of mediocrity that threatens our economic competitiveness globally.

A similar costly mistake that was made to the pre-tertiary institutions is about to be made by the NDC government to the tertiary institutions in Ghana. The government of Ghana intends to elevate all polytechnics in the 10 regions of Ghana, to university status. It appears the NDC administration is not cognizant of the fact that polytechnics fulfill a special role in the economic development of a country. The NDC government is not taking a cue from the experience of the United Kingdom. In 1992, the UK government decided to elevate its polytechnic institutions to university status, only to realize some 22 years later, that the decision was wrong and has now reverted to the status quo.[47]

The government's intention, at a time that the UK government has backtracked based upon its experience in this direction, lays bare the political intentions of the NDC government. Having been unable to deliver on its campaign promises, as a result of massive corruption practices recorded under its watch, the NDC government is desperately trying to find something that would serve as its campaign mantra: that it "elevated" polytechnics to "university" status.

---

[44] Tischler, (1993)

[45] Sakyi, (2011).

[46] Gayton, & Bignold, (2009).

[47] Cockcroft, (2009).

Culture Does Seem to Matter in the
Economic Development of Ghana

It is mind-boggling when one considers the immense natural resources that Ghana is endowed with, yet its people are so trapped in abject poverty and unable to transform those resources into a collective wealth for all its citizens. Developmental economists may prescribe such remedies as implementation of good governance, such as stable political system, encouragement of foreign investment, and corrupt-free and efficient government officials. But it appears that there are more to this than it meets the eye. In fact, rising number of studies[48] suggest that good governance is necessary, but not a sufficient condition for economic development.

A critical missing condition may be cultural values that are suitable for modern business, although these values have not been clearly identified by researchers, probably because of the very challenges inherent in defining culture. But two things in culture that may be hindering this aspiration to national wealth appears to stand clear, which are (a) level of religious beliefs and (b) level of corrupt practices within a group. When these are taken too far, they may become inimical to socio-economic development, irrespective of how naturally resourced a country may be. Natural resources, by themselves, cannot transform into prosperity. It takes people to use them to achieve transformation of those resources into collective wealth. But when a group takes certain beliefs too far, and abandon their identity as the image and likeness of God (Genesis 1:26) or the creator or transformational power of all resources, it is in fact a sin—ignorance of one's identity.

Knowing yourself and your creative capabilities permits you to solve problems in a more pragmatic manner. For example, when the Ghana cedi was determined to be ailing from currency depreciation against major currencies, that implied a problem or a research question had been identified, and the investigation, solution, or healing process should not be any different from approaches used for other scientific inquiry that defines a methodology. Was it a result of inadequate foreign currency reserve, and if so how did that happen? But by merely failing to take these logical steps and simply turning to *praynomics* or praying to command

---

[48]   Hezel, (2014).

the stabilization of a rapidly falling value of the cedi, was amounting to a denial of the implied creative powers that we are told about in Genesis 1:26. In fact, it becomes a replacement of hard work with religiosity, prayer, and preaching, which becomes a mere "substitute for laziness,"[49] and inimical to socio-economic development.

When Fitch Ratings Agency downgraded the creditworthiness of Ghana from a B+ to a B, it utilized certain scientific economic and financial principles. Such principles may be debt-to-equity ratio or how much debt supports asset and labor unrest or strike actions that disrupt economic activities and national production. It utilized similar scientific methodologies to arrive at the conclusion that in 2013, Ghana's current account deficit rose to 12.3% of GDP in 2013, up from an average of 5.7 % in the two years before the 2012's election-related fiscal overspending. This had placed a restriction on the Bank of Ghana's ability to replete the reserves. This was one cause for the rapid depreciation of the cedi.[50] Yet, other people thought they could disregard scientific methodology and prescribe solutions through supernatural methodology for strictly problems of economic nature.

Similarly, when a group aspires to a culture of money-grabbing and corrupt practices, public resources end up enriching private pockets, and does not allow full use of those public resources to help social interventions.

Changing an Aspect of our Culture

An important aspect of Ghana's culture that needs to be supplanted, if we are ever to progress socio-economically, is the inculcation of the spirit of self-dependency. Not very long ago, the president of Ghana was reported as bemoaning the fact that our development partners were not being responsive to our developmental needs."[51] The fact of the matter is that the NDC administration is not acting in tune with the changing times and the international crisis barometer that requires Ghana to utilize its resources with prudence and fiscal discipline. Rather, what the country is seeing

---

49 Otabil, (2014).
50 "Fitch Says Ghana's Massive Rate Hike Alone Unlikely To Support Cedi," (2014).
51 "Our partners ditched us in trying times – Mahama," (2014).

is wanton use and dissipation of state resources through unprecedented acts of corruption in officialdom. The country is still trapped in the mindset that the whole world centers on less developed economies. We tend to think as though the immediate post-independent era mentality of panhandling remains the order of the day in contemporary times and that it would remain so forever. We are acting as though tomorrow will be there forever, instead of using our limited resources to achieve our full potential for present and future generations. Not so anymore, times have changed and keep changing; population has exploded and shrank resources for developed and developing countries alike.

Our developmental partners are themselves going through dynamic change, and we should not expect them to stop for us. They have problems of their own to solve, and it is long past the time that we recognized this new world reality. It is now the time for us to act responsibly with the resources that we have at our disposal, instead of plundering those resources through acts of unprecedented corruption. Probably, the recent inadvertent tweeting from the official American Embassy Twitter account in Ghana was an "honest mistake" intended to draw the attention of Ghana's leadership to the fact that it is about time that the NDC government abandoned rhetoric, imposed financial discipline, and got more serious with Ghana's socio-economic development. After tweeting about Ghana's financial problems and exhorting Ghanaians to make sacrifices, President Mahama received a response from the official US Embassy's Twitter account stating, "And what sacrifices are you making?"[52] Later, however, the Embassy apologized as an "errant tweet" by an embassy staff.

These sentiments of getting Ghana to be self-reliant was also conveyed loud and clear by the NPP flagbearer Nana Akufo-Addo during a discussion about democracy and governance on the BBC Democracy Day held January 20, 2015. Responding to a question from a reporter, Nana Akufo-Addo stated that "one simple truth that all of us on the Continent have to recognise; nobody is going to build this African Continent for us but ourselves."[53]

---

[52] "US embassy apologizes to Ghana leader for tweet," (2014).
[53] The West will never develop Africa - Akufo-Addo," (2015).

The relevance of self-reliance to Ghana's socio-economic development has also been buttressed by the former UN Secretary General, Mr. Kofi Annan. Mr. Annan noted that the international community "can help but they cannot solve the problems for us." This was when Mr. Annan was responding to a question posed by a BBC reporter about the international show of solidarity with French satirical magazine *Charlie Hebdo*, after an attack on its office by an Islamist militant group, which resulted in the loss of the lives of 12 journalists, vis-à-vis the apparent lack of such show of solidarity by the international community on the killing of hundreds of Nigerians in Baga by Islamist militant group Boko Haram, involving close to 2,000 people.[54]

---

[54]   "The West can't solve our problems for us – Kofi Annan tells Africa," (2015).

CHAPTER TWO

Election Disputes and Socio-Economic Development

Culture and colonial legacy, corrupt practices and institutions, and the apparent lack of responsiveness of educational system to economic developmental needs are not the only causes of Ghana's socio-economic woes. In fact, in Ghana's attempts to solve the above problems, it has found itself choosing democratic approach to collective decision making. Such approach to decision making too comes with its own set of problems. The African Union has observed that in as much as elections represent democracy and allow citizens to express their choices about leaders and policies; they also breed conflicts and violence that sometimes threaten the social order and economic development.[55]

This observation by the African Union is amplified by some studies[56] which have observed that political instability is linked with the economic growth of Sub-Saharan African countries. It has been instrumental in sabotaging homegrown efforts to escape a trap revolving around poverty and poor governance. Dubbelman[57] noted that despite strong economic growth over the last decade by African countries, political instability remained an ongoing concern for continued growth. Among the reasons cited for political instability are the lack of well-planned presidential and parliamentary elections and/or lack of a smooth process of handover of power on the eve of political elections.[58]

---

[55] African Union Panel of the Wise. (2010).

[56] Ghura, & Mercereau, (2004); Chimanikire, (2007).

[57] Dubbelman, (2012).

[58] "What are the causes of political instability in Africa?," (2014).

In Ghana, the 2012 presidential and parliamentary elections dispute was finally settled in court, amid skepticism that even the Court's decision was tainted with corruption. Probably, Ghana would have descended into an economically disruptive conflict, were it not for the fact that the contending parties may have been prevailed upon by certain eminent and influential citizens of the country that included two former presidents each from the two dominant and opposing political parties (i.e., the NPP and the NDC); a Roman Catholic Cardinal; and a former UN Secretary General. It is probably appropriate, at this juncture, to review briefly events in Ghana's attempts to solve its conundrum of socio-economic problems through the corridors of democratic approach since 2008, and the significant events that contributed to the "chasing the elephant into the bush."

Background of the 2008 Elections and Subsequent NPP Defeat

Ever since Ghana attained political independence some 58 years ago, sister African countries have demonstrated remarkable interest in both its socio-economic and political developments. Probably, a primary reason may be Ghana's position as the first Sub-Sahara African country to gain political independence, which probably resonates very well with the aspirations of the countries in the sub-region. The 2008 election represented the fifth successive time that Democratic form of national decision making in Ghana was tested, and it held a great significance for other countries especially in the sub-region. The New Patriotic Party or NPP, symbolized by the elephant, and the National Democratic Congress or NDC, symbolized by the umbrella, were the two dominant parties. The leading presidential candidates for these two parties were Nana Akufo-Addo and, now deceased, Prof. John Atta Mills respectively. There were a number of smaller parties as well, totaling six.

The campaigning was earnest, with a number of slogans by each party that were loaded with various sugarplums that each party felt would convey their campaign promises and messages to attract sizeable segments of the voters. For example, the NPP's "we are moving forward and the NDC's "Change you can trust" were among some of the slogans. The last day of campaigning witnessed major rallies by the two dominant parties. Women's representation, especially at the parliamentary level, was high on the agenda of this election. A number of international organizations such as, Convention on the Elimination of all Forms of Discrimination against Women and Beijing Platform for Action were very much supportive of this agenda. However, this agenda was met with some disappointment, as the number of parliamentary seats won by women fell below expectations.

Intervention measures against possibility of violence, such as peace walks, peace songs, billboards depicting the harsh realities of refugee life, and the broadcast of peace messages from distinguished citizens were organized to preach the message of peace across the length and breadth of Ghana, were implemented. The election was very close, with the NPP obtaining 49.1% of the valid votes cast, and the NDC obtaining 47.96%, both parties falling short of the constitutional requirement of 50% + 1 vote to secure a first round victory. This meant a runoff that saw intense criss-crossings in the country by functionaries of both the NPP and the NDC. In the end, Prof. John Atta Mills, the NDC flagbearer, was declared the winner by a margin of less than 1% or 40,586 votes.[59] Probably, it was the closest election in a region where campaign violence is often sparked after announcements. It was a big plus for Ghana, and as then President Kufuor remarked, even though it was very close, it did not really merit any dispute that may carry a risk of violence.

While it was the wish of the majority of Ghanaians that harmony would prevail, the experience of other African states was enough to put the electorate on edge. For example, the polling day in Kenya was quiet and smooth; it was the refusal of either of the big parties to concede to loss that sparked the violence. In the case of Ghana, the closeness of the results made both parties scramble feverishly for every vote to win the second round. This was where violence is usually triggered.

The Mistakes of the NPP

Ever since the elephant was chased out of the city into the bush in 2008, the city has been beset by severe economic problems. The first scheduled

---

[59] "Ghanaian general election, 2008," (2015).

attempt to return the elephant into the city was 2012. By several accounts, many reasons contributed to the elephant's defeat that led to it being chased out into the bush. Some reasons why the NPP lost the 2008 elections came from many members of the party such as Mr. Mustapha Hamid and Dr. Arthur Kennedy, who even wrote a book titled, *Chasing the Elephant into the Bush*, which has served as a progenitor of the title of this book. A number of feature articles attempted to shift the blame away from party executives and the campaign team of Nana Akufo-Addo and lay it on the doorstep of former President Kufuor. Other writers, such as John Musah who claimed to be neither a sympathizer of the elephant nor the umbrella parties, but a committed citizen of Ghana whose sole motivation for offering his opinion was to help deepen the advancement of multi-party democracy in the country, cited several reasons why the elephant lost to the umbrella. According to Musah, some of the incidences that contributed to the elephant's defeat in 2008 are presented below:

Campaign Team Caliber: Bragging and Ostentatious Lifestyle

The NPP overlooked the caliber of people who made up their campaign teams. According to Musah,[60] there were isolated cases of some campaign team members who often came from Accra to the North to campaign exhibiting unacceptable behaviors that did cost the NPP significant votes. Musah noted that they would come from Accra and stay in expensive hotels, always eager to mention and stress on the hotels they were staying to insinuate some kind of status to impress the local folks. They would go to the drinking bars and talk big, snap their fingers in arrogance, order expensive drinks, and go after other people's women. Musah further noted that the young members of the NPP campaign team in the North too did not help matters. They bragged and went after other peoples' girlfriends with their campaign cash. For example, they would collect curriculum vitae (CV) of acquaintances in the North with the pretext of helping them find jobs when they won the elections and later dump them in their campaign pickup trucks. They would then show such CVs to the ladies bragging, "don't mind him, that is even his CV, he has been bothering me to find him a job." The whole objective was to enable them gain access into their bodies whenever they came down to the North. The youth in the

---

[60]   Musah, (2009).

North witnessed and discussed such incidences. It was a political suicide that particularly did cost the NPP a hell lot of the youth votes in the North. The NPP was simply over-confident of winning the elections "one touch" and humility was completely missing.

Musah went on to note that people were complaining and sometimes even wondered whether those campaigners really meant business of winning the elections, or whether the NPP campaign had a research and monitoring team on the ground that cautioned those irresponsible campaign team members. There was also the problem of timing with regards to certain decisions that the elephant party took. For example, the purchase of the presidential jet, building of the presidential palace, and the last minute rush decisions to reduce fuel prices after round one, which particularly was perceived by the voters as signs of desperation. However, time has demonstrated that some of those perceived "ostentatious lifestyles," such as the presidential jet and presidential palace did not truly merit those perceived "ostentatious" lifestyles classification. After all, today, the NDC government is comfortably enjoying those very amenities for which it bitterly criticized the NPP government, and worked so hard to make the voters tune in to their perceived "ostentatious lifestyle." The NPP campaign simply failed to communicate effectively to the voters about the necessity for the acquisition of those facilities, and probably too, as I stated earlier, the timing was just not right. Nevertheless, there was some extent of extravagance by the NPP that should have been monitored closely by the research and information gathering team to provide campaign strategists facts on the ground. For example, one observer noted the number of musicians the NPP campaign paid to criss-cross the country with them, the big Ford vehicles with heavily mounted musical systems, and the expensive billboards everywhere. It, indeed, had elements of "politics of complacency" but they were inextricable part of the natural behavior of an incumbent party's political campaign. The funds were simply available. Hopefully, as the 2016 election campaign gathers steam, the NPP campaign will be guided by experience and avoid repeat of such pitfalls.

Plain Old Corruption

Another factor that might have also contributed to the NPP's defeat was the issue of alleged corruption. After eight years in power, the level of corruption, be it real or perceived, had become too high. For example, it became so glaring to come by many individuals who owed no properties, prior to NPP coming into power, but suddenly turning to be owners of mansions and expensive cars. This in itself, may not be a bad achievement, after all, that is a natural human aspiration provided they were not acquired at the expense of the taxpayers. But the revulsion aspect, and the worst of all, is the way those individuals flaunted those newly-acquired wealth right in the face of the voters.

CHAPTER THREE

Election 2012 and the Unfinished Contract with Ghana

Background of the 2012 Elections

This election occurred under very unusual circumstances. About five months to the election, the sitting President John Atta-Mills died, leaving his Vice-President, John Mahama, to be sworn in as president under constitutional provision. This election took place on 7th December 2012 to elect a president and members of parliament in 275 electoral constituencies.[61] As a result of the breakdown of some biometric verification machines, some voters could not vote, and voting was extended by another day.[62] This decision received a broad welcome by both political parties and voters, who hoped the poll would further deepen Ghana's credentials as a beacon of democracy in a region prone to civil wars, coups, corruption, and election violence.

The umbrella party, under incumbent John Mahama was declared winner of the election with 50.7% of the vote, just a few thousand votes above the threshold for avoiding a run-off election. Nana Akufo-Addo received 47.74%.[63] The elephant party detected vote tampering by the Electoral Commission (EC) and filed a petition at the Supreme Court to review the election results. In a separate part of the procedure, the EC was challenged to prove that 14,000 expatriate Ghanaians had voted abroad. But the EC

---

[61]   Electoral Commission of Ghana, (2012).
[62]   "Ghana extends voting to Saturday after technical hitch," (2012).
[63]   "Ghana Election: John Mahama declared winner," (2012).

was unable to produce any registered voters in foreign countries, claiming that a computer virus had corrupted files on that record.[64]

In spite of the declarations by international observers, including the Coalition of Domestic Election Observers (CODEO), the Economic Community of West African States (ECOWAS) and the African Union (AU) that the elections were, for the most part, free and fair the NPP still harbored deep-seated feelings that it was otherwise.[65]

Nature of the Unfinished Contract with Ghana

The contract with Ghana is an implied adherence and commitment to certain systematic public policies that aims at quickening the pace of Ghana's socio-economic development for which a political party is elected into office to prosecute. It involves fiscal discipline, probity, and accountability in governance to permit resources to be channeled to where they are most needed, such as education, health, roads, water, energy, and agricultural sectors. The terms of this contract were largely kept by the NPP government, as evidenced by the stabilization in most of the macroeconomic indicators between 2000 and 2008.[66] However, from 2008 to date, this contract has witnessed neglect, stagnation, and non-performance for nearly seven years under the NDC administration, as evidenced by unprecedented borrowings that are not being felt in the economy or without any projects to show.[67] It is imperative now that the contract be revived and performed by the NPP for the true well-being of all Ghanaians. The two main vehicles of this contract for achieving rapid socio-economic development are education for the citizenry and corruption-free leadership. Lack of education and enlightenment breed ignorance and naïve citizens, who are unable to scrutinize effectively developmental policies and are easily preyed upon by some politicians and some religious leaders who swindle them out of their rights. Corruption is evidenced by weak and ineffective social institutions that

---

[64]   Wikipedia, "Ghanaian general election 2012." (2015).

[65]   "Ghana election: NPP considers challenge to John Mahama win," (2012).

[66]   "NDC govt practising 'Akonfem socialism' – Bawumia," (2013).

[67]   Ibid.

allow misdirection of public resources for socio-economic development, and accrue only to the benefits of private and few individual interests.

In a BBC report in the 2012 election campaign,[68] Nana Akufo-Addo of the NPP vowed to provide free SHS education and root out corruption. In fact, a larger extent of the causes of Ghana's socio-economic under-development lies in education and corruption, and the two constitute the primary agenda of the unfinished contract. Fix education and corruption problems and you have solved Ghana's socio-economic problems, or at least, made a significant headway in that direction. So, what does solving the education problem or the free SHS education really imply? That after the free SHS head start, beneficiaries would be able to progressively better understand and critically analyze social institutions, public policy, think independently and creatively to foster socio-economic development. In a similar vein, what really is corruption that has continuously dominated the conversation on socio-economic development? It is that plague that publicly, everyone shuns but privately the darling of a significant number of people. I am going to attempt to relate how education can enhance our comprehension of certain issues, and how corruption can be minimized to permit Ghana to move forward together in the socio-economic front.

Education

The PPP presidential candidate, Dr. Paa Kwesi Nduom, recently observed that "uneducated people tend to be poor and are easily deceived by politicians, social and religious leaders and employers. One sure path to prosperity is to make education a right and to make government responsible for ensuring that all citizens get a minimum level of formal education. Compulsory education is the answer and is necessary for Ghana to become a great and strong nation."[69] Thomas Jefferson, the third President of the United States, is credited as noting that "Enlighten the people generally, and tyranny and oppressions of body and mind will vanish like evil spirits at the dawn of day." Education enables a society to respond to the politico-economic processes and to stay competitive. This perspective on education is shared and lauded the world over. For example, as recently as January 2015, US President Obama was reported

---

[68] "Ghana extends voting to Saturday after technical hitch," (2012).
[69] "Compulsory education will make Ghana great, strong," (2015).

as proposing that the first two years of community college education should be "free for everybody who's willing to work for it."[70]

But what is education that the whole world seems to be singing its praises? Is education simply the ability to read and write? If education was simply the ability to read and write, then all the foreign aid with conditions for SSA states, including Ghana, aimed at amending the North-South economic disparity should have yielded dramatic results by now because they were administered by people who could read and write. True education must carry the ultimate purpose of selfless service to society where, as John F. Kennedy rightly noted, citizens rather ask what they can do to help their country, and not what their country can help them acquire. Because this kind of education is absent today in Ghana, we see "a breakdown of discipline and a stifling of the spirit of selflessness in our society."[71] This true education begins with formal education, and goes beyond the mere provision of credentials.

The NPP realized that to achieve the education that carries the ultimate purpose of selfless service to the society, it must begin with free education at the SHS level to create enlightened citizenry in the country as enjoined by the 1992 Constitution of Ghana. The fact is, one must be equipped with reading and critical reasoning skills to be able to analyze public policy issues and understand certain concepts involved in social institutions such as religion, before gradually being led into the ultimate and true meaning of education—selfless service to society. A byproduct of this ultimate goal of education or the true meaning of education, where corruption and money-grabbing tendencies become more subdued within the individual, is the attainment of academic skills to function effectively as adults. These skills include the ability to hold down a job, balance a checkbook, evaluate political candidates, read a newspaper, be able to understand the import of social institutions, and analyze the importance of a scientific study in this time of global competition. With a literacy rate of 71.5% for Ghanaians 15 years and older (for a population of about 25 million as at 2010) who can read and write, there is adequate room for vulnerability and naivety for exploitation by certain groups of people who may want to exploit the ignorant for selfish interest.

---

[70] Essert, (2015).
[71] "Rawlings angry at current state of affairs," (2015).

The remaining 28.5% of the people are either illiterate or semi-literate. That is, we may have a situation in Ghana where the teacher, a semi-literate, may be instructing the student, completely illiterate. By teacher, I mean both the teacher in the secular world and teacher in the religious world. The activities of some of those so-called religious teachers or pastors leave much to be desired, and it appears some of them just prey on the naivety of the uneducated, as they pursue their own self-interests of money-grabbing. For example, Article 21 Clause (1) subsection (c) of the 1992 Ghana Constitution reads: "All persons shall have the right to freedom to practice any religion and to manifest such practice" and Article 12 Clause (2) of the 1992 Ghana constitution reads: "Every person in Ghana, whatever his race, place of origin, political opinion, color, religion, creed or gender shall be entitled to the fundamental human rights and freedoms of the individual contained in this Chapter but subject to respect for the rights and freedoms of others and for the public interest."

While the Constitution guarantees freedom of religion, it makes such guarantees of freedom contingent on and subjected to the respect for the rights and freedoms of others for the public interest. Not long ago, in this regard, a so-called pastor was seen in a video stomping repeatedly on the belly of a pregnant woman purposely in a prayer of deliverance. Unfortunately, there are always those members of society who are gullible, vulnerable, and preyed upon by people who claim to have extraordinary spiritual powers. They are preyed upon because they are illiterate, ignorant, disabled, and are unable to read and decipher the codes of religion. Sometimes, the predator is semi-literate and equally disabled, and having a blunt or unrefined conscience. In the case of this so-called pastor, the pregnant woman's right was clearly being subjected to disrespect in the name of the pastor's religious freedom. This is a clear example of where true education for the people causes ignorance to "vanish like evil spirits at the dawn of day" that Thomas Jefferson referred to.

The intent and purpose of religion has often been misconstrued by some ill-trained and so-called "men of God" and is now becoming a real problem in Ghana. There is now proliferation of religion to the extent that numerous small churches now engulf every community in Ghana. Religion has clearly been misunderstood by some and is being utilized by others as tools to maximize personal wealth. The solution: educate the people and lift them up above vulnerability, gullibility, and ignorance.

Literacy helps to lift the veil that permits explanation and understanding of certain concepts in the 21st century. Let us visit, for example, the cases of two public figures: one a prominent religious leader, who resorted to "prayers to command the stabilization" of the rapidly declining value of the Ghanaian currency against world major currencies, and the other who was alleged to have attributed the cause of the rapidly declining level of the country's major currency reserves and the concomitant depreciation of the cedi to 'voodoo' or spiritual forces.[72] These raise the question of the impact of misconstrued forms of religion and animism mentality, which have become the bane of Ghana's socio-economic development. After all, the Bible explicitly states that faith that is not supported by practical work and effort is dead (James 2: 17, 20, 26). It implies that irrespective of how religious Ghanaians may be, the people can never see the light of any economic transformation if they don't start a process of practical change of attitude and stop clinging to the wrong and uninformed kind of prayers that solely rely on utterances of words to God.[73]

To understand the import of *praynomics,* as this public leader's "prayers to command the stabilization" of the cedi has come to be known, it may be appropriate to review the role of religion in human life. Religion has been an excellent servant for social control and security throughout antiquity, long before contemporary policing techniques evolved as tool for social control and security. Yet paradoxically, it has often appeared as one of the very instruments of divisiveness and instability in society. An example of its divisiveness and instability was demonstrated in the political situation in Iraq, where the ruling Shiite Islam majority were less inclined to include the minority Sunni Islam in political decision making largely because of the absence of group identity and solidarity, which has culminated in an insurgency.[74]

---

[72]   Adeniran, (2014).
[73]   "Religious prayers useless for Ghana, Africa's transformation – Fifi Kwetey," (2014).
[74]   Tawfeeq, Smith-Spark, & Carter, (2014).

Nature and elements of religion.

Undoubtedly, I do have my highest regard and tolerance for diversity in religion or the conceptualization of God. I am also quite cognizant of the possible fact that in this very diversity, there emerges, God the Almighty and the creator of heaven and earth. I also happen to believe that one of the purposes that human beings were created in physical form is for the Creator to allow us an avenue to encounter for numerous times the reality of experience that will try the soul's strength on. In fulfilling this purpose, it makes ample sense that we live together on earth as brothers and sisters and be each other's keeper. One researcher[75] defined religion as "a system of beliefs, practices and philosophical values shared by a group of people that defines the sacred, helps explain life, and provides salvation from the problems of human existence."

The importance of religion, therefore, in the life of the human being cannot be overemphasized. Every religion has adopted its own formalized social rituals such as prayer, with slight variations in the activities that comprise those rituals, as individual members of a religion engage in prayer supplication with the supernatural beings or forces that transcend human capabilities or God. For example, some apostolic churches in Ghana claim to "speak in tongues" during their prayer rituals, often rambling in utterances that may appear meaningless to other people. From the perspective of Machiavelli, religion was that element necessarily subordinate to the state and a necessary component of national life; because it may be a powerful tool in governance that keeps human beings subdued. To Machiavelli, human beings were by nature lawless and unfaithful, and religion was some kind of social control that imposed fear of eternal punishment in the subjects in order to increase their great respect for the decrees of the state. And, as long as religion performed this function, its authenticity was unquestionable, and believed that religion was a necessary complement of good laws and military power that constitute the bedrock of national life.[76]

---

[75]   Tischler, (1993).
[76]   Vergani, (1997).

The inner and the outer religions.

Likening the inner and the outer religions to the *Allegory of the Cave in* Plato's *Republic* that depicted contemporary condition of the human being, one writer[77] elucidated on a central concept in religion. This concept has been proven by modern research as a notion that has characterized all major religions from times of antiquity. Three prisoners had been chained inside the cave all their life under conditions and reality that allowed them to see only false images and shadows of objects. Then as one is sent outside the cave and sees new reality for the first time, he returns to tell his experience, but to his dismay, the other prisoners inside the cave do not believe his fantastic stories of the world outside of the cave. The central concept pertains to Moses' encounter with the burning bush (Exodus 3: 14), and the announcement of the "I am that I am." It was the present tense of the verb "To be" in its indicative mood, announcement of a "Being" in the absolute state or that first originating plane of pure spirit where, because of the non-existent physical nature of the material, there can neither be any extension in space nor sequence in time. Under such conditions, it could only exist in self-consciousness form, with no limitation either of time or space which till this time of Moses, was an exclusive secret of the inner religion. What then did this imply? Pure spirit is the ultimate essence of all that is, and hence "All-livingness," All-presence," "All-knowledge," and "All-lovingness" of God. Then as a corollary of the proposition that "spirit is the ultimate essence of *all* that exists," there must be the converse proposition that "*All* that exist, is spirit." Herein is derived human beings as the image and likeness of God in Genesis 1:26. So symbolisms that manifested in the outer religions were used to convey this central concept because not all individuals had the nous to make this final deduction. This notion of God, the "I am that I am," was noted by Pope Benedict XVI in his speech at the University of Regensburg, Germany, on September 12, 2006[78] as "a profound encounter between faith and reason, ... encounter between genuine enlightenment and religion."

But it takes some level of education to grasp such concepts, and that is why the NPP is bent on free SHS education for all, so that people can

---

[77]   Troward, (2012).

[78]   "Full text of Benedict's XVI's speech in Germany," (2006).

better understand and analyze social institutions and public policy within the confines of their own refined intellect. Otherwise, ignorance will continue to persist among a significant number of Ghanaians.

Corruption

Publicly, everyone perceives and talks about corruption as though, it was a plague or some kind of contagious disease that must be shunned by all. But privately, the picture is probably different. Many people even embrace and kiss corruption in the closet because no one sees them. It really does make some of us hypocrites. Otumfuo Osei Tutu II aptly summed up the nature of corruption in his "corruption carousel" remark as a guest speaker at the 19th Ghana Journalists Association Awards in 2014 that "we are all on what I call a corruption carousel."[79] Someone also likened corruption to salt: there is a little amount of it in any tasty meal. But too much becomes dangerous and steals away the tastiness of the meal.

Unfortunately, similar to a human shadow, corruption has followed the human being ever since the time of creation. It has, however, assumed more prominence in contemporary times as technological advancement, with its deluge of products and services available for sale feeds the frenzy of corruption. The numerous products and services on the market of contemporary times are swaying consumers demand in unprecedented levels. Whereas in the earlier times, there were fewer products and services; today we have numerous products out there in the market. For example, some thirty years ago, mobile phones, flat screen color TVs, personal computers, and a whole array of electronic products were all unheard of. Today many people own one, purchased with money. So our basic needs have expanded from food, clothing, and shelter to now include those new products on the market. Even the basic needs of food, clothing, and shelter have come with their own innovations, making them much more expensive. How do the millions of people satisfy the numerous wants? The answer is corruption--to raise the needed funds to purchase those goods and services.

---

[79] "Ghana On A Corruption Carousel," (2014).

To be fair, corruption is unfortunately a part and parcel of human life if only one could get away with it. Very few people can be exempted from the "corruption carousel." So, the question is: how do we deter and control corruption so that it doesn't siphon off public funds that could, otherwise, be used to achieve transformational effect on the socio-economic front? How do we deter and control corruption so that it doesn't undermine investor confidence and drive away the much needed investments into the country for socio-economic development? How do we deter and control corruption so that the public official doesn't compromise state and public interest for his or her own parochial interest? US President Obama gave us the answer—strong institutions, not strong men. Not strong men with guns pointed at corrupt officials and citizens 24/7. Strong men don't last; but strong institutions backed by good laws do.

Some of us were privileged to have witnessed the early times of the PNDC regime in 1982, when guns held at bay corruption tendencies, to some extent, by making its practice a dangerous undertaking. In fact, several people lost their lives even if one was merely suspected or perceived to be engaging in any corrupt behavior. Citizens Vetting Committees (CVCs) were established and empowered to investigate people whose lifestyle and expenditure substantially exceeded their known incomes. Specifically, anyone with more than ¢50,000 (US$1,250 at the prevailing black market exchange rate of some ¢50 to a US$) were invited to appear before the CVC to explain how they acquired it, with the wealthy becoming the targets of a vindictive Public Tribunal system. The situation was so intimidating that it became not uncommon for some people to dispose of their cash, especially of higher denominations, into the incinerator. Fast track to today, what do we see under the NDC government's watch? Corruption has been given a free rein. There is so much corruption in public places that today, a whole new phrase has even been coined for it in public officialdom -- create, loot, and share. An example of this phrase can be illustrated in a recent scenario between the NDC government and the World Bank where the government contracted a World Bank loan of US$154 million on behalf of Ghana (create); announced its intention to apportion certain percentage of the loan in the amount of US$15 million to purchase sanitary pads for all girls in second cycle institutions (loot); with possible end result of distributing some of the US$15 million among party cronies (share).

So, the propensity to engage in corrupt practices can only be held in check through strong institutions and anti-corruption laws designed to provide for the prevention, investigation, and punishment of corruption. Strong institutions and anti-corruption laws serve as deterrent against the desire to engage in corrupt practices, and together with good laws and enforcement, the problem of corruption can be very well contained or reduced to the barest minimum. For example, in Kenya and some states in the US, there are pension forfeiture laws that basically provide that upon conviction of certain corruption offenses, some public servants forfeit their right to receive pension benefits or a portion thereof for breaching the public trust. Perhaps we can learn from those countries' experiences in dealing with corruption in Ghana.

Given the endemic nature of corruption in the Ghanaian culture, any attempt by any government to enact serious laws that will militate against corruption is likely to be privately unpopular with most people at the initial stages. But failure to pursue such course of action or get the country to swallow the bitter pill will stifle the country's socio-economic development, and perhaps indefinitely.

This writer happened to witness an interesting part of a conversation between an NDC sympathizer and an NPP sympathizer that touched on the theme of corruption and the impending 2016 elections. The conversation went like this:

> **NDC Sympathizer:** "...So, do you think there's anybody here in Ghana who is corrupt-free in Ghanaian politics? Where is your assurance that Nana Akufo-Addo can fight corruption in Ghana? Look, this is the modus operandi: assume you're the minister or the head in a state organization that intends to award a contract worth GH¢100 million. A businessman who wants the contract with your organization visits you in your house and says: 'Here are the keys and lease to your two 3-bedroom houses at East Legon and Ahodwo in Kumasi, all in your name. Here also are your keys to the brand new Toyota 4 x 4 Land Cruiser vehicle parked outside at the front door to this house,' and the businessman drops them on your sitting room center table. 'Please approve that

bid for me,' and he leaves the documents in your possession adding, 'Let me hear from you,' and walks away. What will you do? Are you going to turn the infallible angel? There is nobody, and absolutely nobody in Ghana who has the will to fight corruption! So you can't trust any political party. You're better off leaving the NDC to continue ruling the country," he expressed himself forcefully.

NPP Sympathizer: "Okay, you can't trust anybody and any political party to be corrupt-free in Ghana politics, right? But in Ghana politics, there is such a thing as once a party spends two terms of eight years; it has to move on and create opportunity for another group of *corrupt* politicians, as you yourself just noted okay? In spite of Kufuor's NPP legacy of free National Health Insurance and positioning the country for favorable investment climate and economic development, the party was shown the exit to the opposition chamber in 2008. Why? His party's two terms of eight years was up. It was the same with Rawlings' NDC. Ghana's politics is largely driven by change, after two terms, irrespective of your accomplishments, you must go."

The NDC sympathizer was now silent. He had been trounced in his home turf, by weapons of his own beliefs and logic in corruption. Later, the NPP sympathizer told this writer that there was no way he could sway the NDC sympathizer to his side to understand that indeed, there were people who really believed in "good name is better than riches," and are genuinely concerned with the well being of current citizens and future generation. So the only way he could get it into his NDC interlocutor's head was to use his own premises, logic, and belief which were the "corrupt nature of politicians" argument.

CHAPTER FOUR

Decision 2016: The Way Forward

The Fatal Blunders under the NDC government

The Ghana Government is publicly committed to minimizing the practice of corruption by government officials. However, official salaries are relatively modest, especially for low-level staff. There have been recorded instances of certain employees asking clients for tips in return for assisting them with jobs for which they are paid to do. The 1992 Constitution of Ghana supported the provision of a Commission on Human Rights and Administrative Justice (CHRAJ). Among its functions, the Commission has the responsibility to investigate all instances of alleged and suspected corruption and the misappropriation of public funds by officials and individuals in their dealings with the state. The Commission also has authority to take appropriate initiatives, including providing reports to the Attorney General and the Auditor-General, in connection with such investigations. It is also within the mandate of the Commission to prosecute alleged violations when there is sufficient evidence to initiate legal actions. The Commission, however, is under-resourced and not many prosecutions have been made since it was established. In 1998, the Government of Ghana also established an anti-corruption institution, called the Serious Fraud Office (SFO) charged with the responsibility to investigate corrupt practices involving both private and public institutions. Even though the government has announced plans to streamline the roles of the CHRAJ and SFO, with the goal of eliminating duplication of functions, they have not successfully impacted on corruption.[80]

Laws and institutions without enforcement are only as good as without them. It appears that Ghana is very good at imitating the Western type of

---

[80]   Wikipedia, "Corruption in Ghana," (2015).

institutions, replete with well-crafted function descriptions in books, but those good laws and institutions are not so good when it comes to their practice in Ghana. Such condition facilitates the use of not only officialdom for personal financial gains, but also just about every individual in the system. There have been a number of high profile cases of corruption and financial improprieties under the watch of the NDC government. These cases have, no doubt, incurred voter revulsion towards the NDC government, as they perceive in those corruption cases the government's tacit support. Among this high profile corruption cases are:

Woyome Judgment Debt Scandal

On February 7, 2012, it was reported that four prominent supporters of the NDC had been arrested and charged with corruption in an Accra court. In that respect, Alfred Agbesi Woyome was charged with crimes, including corrupting public officials in a multi-million dollar payment that a government inquiry alleged he had claimed illegally. Likewise, Chief Attorney Samuel Neequaye-Tetteh, his wife and the Finance Ministry's Legal Director were also charged with aiding and abetting a crime.

Woyome was charged with defrauding Ghana by false pretenses and causing financial loss to the state, in the amount of GH¢51.2 million or about US$30 million at that time. State prosecutors claimed Mr. Woyome, in February 2010, made a false representation that the government owed him two per cent of €1,106,470,587 for his services of financial engineering for the rehabilitation of the Kumasi, Accra, and El-Wak stadia, ahead of the CAN 2008 African Cup of Nations. At the time, accusations were leveled against the President John Atta Mills that he was soft on corruption. An investigation into the payments found that Woyome had made false claims. According to a report, the Attorney General at the time and later appointed as Minister of Education, Mrs. Betty Mould Iddrisu, was linked to the decision to pay GH¢51.2 million to Woyome over a construction deal he said was wrongly terminated. The new Attorney General, Mr. Martin Amidu, accused some cabinet ministers of "gargantuan crimes against the state," and his appointment was suddenly terminated by Atta-Mills. Iddrisu resigned her position as the Minister of Education. But, the sacked Amidu, affectionately referred to as "citizen vigilante," went ahead with the case against Woyome and won it. However, the money is yet to be refunded to the taxpayer of Ghana.[81]

Ghana Youth Employment and Entrepreneurial Development Agency (GYEEDA)

The GYEEDA corruption scandal made the national headlines in April 2013, when public pressure forced the NDC government to constitute a committee to probe an alleged maladministration and financial misappropriation at the agency. The outcome of the committee's report attested to the fact of certain violations of state laws, and from the report those violations appeared to have been facilitated with the assistance of officialdom.

More specifically, among what the investigations revealed are the following[82]:

1. The head of finance at GYEEDA had admitted that he did not have the requisite qualification for the position he was appointed.
2. From 2008-2012, no financial statements or budgets were ever prepared.
3. The agency lacked internal audit control.
4. From the period 2009-2012, GYEEDA received GH¢949,661,017 from five unauthorized sources (i.e., the District Assembly Common Fund, GETFUND, NHIS, Ministry of Finance and Economic Planning, and Communication Service Tax) to finance unspecified projects. Those funding sources increased at an alarming rate. For example, in 2009, total funding was GH¢115,260,000; it grew to GH¢157,341,000in 2010. By 2011, it had increased to GH¢228,015,437, and in the election year 2012, the funding surged to GH¢449,044,580.
5. By 2013, GYEEDA also owed an additional GH¢259,000,000. Of this amount, alleged debt of GH¢122,000,000 was supposed to be owed to a company called Better Ghana Management Service Limited (BGMS). According to the report, not only did all the management team members of GYEEDA resist the BGMS

---

[81] "Four of Ghana's ruling elite charged with corruption," (2012).
[82] "The GYEEDA Report: Interactive Summary," (2014).

engagement, but also it turned out that GYEEDA was paying an unreasonable financing cost of about 100% per month or 1,200% per annum on this debt.

6. The business model of GYEEDA called for doing business with Service Providers that allowed it to transfer national resources to these Service Providers for little or no value received. The Service Providers for GYEEDA projects were heavily skewed in favor of certain individuals. There were certain individuals who owned more than eight GYEEDA contracts at a time with aggregate contract values in excess of GH¢150,000,000.

7. The typical procedure for these Service Providers was to generate unsolicited bid, which invariably was approved by GYEEDA's management or in some cases by obscure politically connected hands. Once the contract was executed, the funds were released to the Service Providers even before work was done.

8. From 2009 -2012, GYEEDA paid approximately GH¢786,000,000 to Service Providers as contractual claims.

9. Several of the contracts between GYEEDA and the Service Providers lacked basic standard elements of contracts such as critical dates, deliverables, tenure, and key performance indicators.

10. The Office of the Attorney General and Minister of Justice were left out from the execution of many of these contracts.

Savannah Accelerated Development Authority (SADA)

SADA was established in 2010 to assist in expediting development in the northern sector of Ghana. It is governed by an independent Board of Directors appointed by the President. Government gave the Authority an initial capital of GH¢25 million as part of a move to help a Development Fund that was established for the project to grow. SADA seeks funds of up to US$145 million to execute its mandate. SADA's jurisdiction comprises the three regions in the north of Ghana, namely, Upper East, Upper West and the Northern Region. It stretches to include districts located in the north of Brong Ahafo and Volta regions. SADA forms part of Ghana's policy response to the widening effects of climate change associated with floods and draught in the north of Ghana. It also aims at alleviating poverty in the northern parts of the country.

However, an Auditor-General's report found several adverse financial improprieties that public pressure has mounted on President John Mahama to intervene to prove his commitment in the fight against corruption. But to date, nothing has come out of it. The Auditor-General's report[83] found the following:

1. GH¢1,059,649.00 went into what the report called "inappropriate mode of selecting consultants" for SADA. The report noted that under the Public Procurement Act 663 of 2003, consultants should be selected based upon capabilities and resources to perform their assignments, but the SADA management ignored that critical requirement.

2. SADA had employed the services of highly skilled professionals who were well remunerated to carry out their assignments. Yet, management contracted four consultants that it paid them monthly fees totaling GH¢620,206.00 while SADA management failed to produce the profiles and performance reports on the activities of the consultants to enable them to assess their effectiveness.

3. A Resource Mobilization Consultant, for instance, failed to generate any revenue for the Authority since his first appointment in January 2013. However, his contract had been renewed for another six months, which the report noted was "a drain on the financial resources of the Authority that is meant to alleviate poverty within the SADA zone."

4. SADA management "engaged the consultants currently providing services to the Authority without going through public advertisement to ensure that people with the right caliber were selected," and that the "audit team could not even sight the profile of the consultants providing services to SADA, which "blurred transparency and could compromise value for money and for that matter facilitate financial abuse."

5. The Auditor General "noticed that the management spent a whopping £279,684.76 (equivalent of GH¢839,054.28) and GH¢364,594.76 totaling GH¢1,203,649.04 on consultancy services during the period under review."

---

[83] Owusu, (2014).

$3 million Airlift to Brazil for the Black Stars Team

This action represented the pinnacle of unacceptable behavior by a modern day government -- the NDC government. There was nothing wrong in paying the players money and allowances that was rightfully due them. But to airlift such huge amount of money, in this day of electronic funds transfer, was at once another clear example of the "create, loot, and share" agenda of the NDC government. It not only helped some people in the government to misappropriate state funds, but also it created a conflict with patriotism. If there is any conspicuous and common ritual that is observed in any FIFA World Cup event, that ritual is unmistakably the playing of national anthems of competing teams' countries right before the start of each game. It kindles the spirit of patriotism and flares up loyalty and valor to go forth into battle without any mortal fear, in hopes of winning the battle for one's country.

A number of studies[84] have noted that generally, patriotism connotes attachment or devotion to one's country, having some kind of a close relationship with nationalism. Often, the name patriotism is invoked whenever a group of people faces a common enemy such as in military warfare, in sporting games, or even in domestic political rivalry activities. Thus, the ennobling effects of sacrifice and duty are relevant in both times of war and of peace; the sense of common sacrifices for nation obligate the citizens just as security agents make in the name of national defense and stability. The same is expected of entrepreneurs to make for the future and economic development of a country, and academic researchers contribute to the legacy of science and economic development. Surprisingly, policy makers in Ghana appeared to have lost their direction during the FIFA World Cup games in Brazil.

The airlift of US$3 million to Brazil to pay a team that was representing the country in the world cup was clearly a direct challenge and an affront to patriotism. It exposed the country to international ridicule, especially when the Brazil government saw the opportunity to tax 17% on each player's income of US$100,000 as appearance fees. Probably, it was even more of a ridicule given that this airlift of US$3 million occurred at a time that the country was panhandling for US$156 million from the

---

[84]   Blatberg, (2000); Calhoun, (2004).

World Bank to support community Day Senior High School program,[85] despite Ghana's share of oil revenue of GH¢690.26 million (US$444.12 million) and GH¢978.27 million (US$541.07 million) for 2011 and 2012 respectively.[86] As one academician rightfully observed, "it was 'absolutely incompetent' for government to superintend over such a scandal,"[87] not to mention the negative signals it transmitted to patriotism.

The real reason why this could occur is that, as someone succinctly wrote, "Never forget that public ignorance is the government's best friend." Probably, a series of "Red Fridays" and "Occupy Judiciary-Executive-Legislature (OJEL)" will begin to make it read, "Never forget that public enlightenment is the government's worst enemy." That is why the NPP is committed to reducing such public ignorance through free SHS education that became its campaign slogan in the 2012 Election season. That is why the NPP deserves to be given a chance in 2016 to prosecute the unfinished contract with Ghana.

Amatefe Drug Trafficking Scandal

Just as things were beginning to subside a little bit, another case that appeared to have the hallmark of connivance and collaboration of public officials in the NDC government surfaced in the Ghanaian media on November 10, 2014. This time, it was an attempt to smuggle about 12.5 kg of cocaine into the United Kingdom by a 32-years-old Ghanaian lady who goes by aliases, including Nayele Amatefe, Ruby Adu-Gyamfi and Angel. She was arrested in the United Kingdom and was sentenced on January 5, 2015 by the Isleworth Crown Court in the United Kingdom to 8 years and 8 months imprisonment. It was reported that she and two others breached Ghana's airport security allegedly with the assistance of three Ghanaian Security and Foreign Affairs officials. Nayele and her two accomplices were reported to have used the VVIP section of the Kotoka International Airport (KIA), an area reserved for the president and high-ranking government officials only, to board a British Airways flight. Her two female accomplices escaped in London but were arrested on their return to Ghana, and later acquitted by a court. Ametefe pleaded guilty

---

85   "Full details of govt's $156 Million Loan," (2014).

86   "Ghana Crude Oil Revenue," (2014).

87   Gadugah, (2014).

to the offense of drug trafficking and implored the UK judge to speed up her sentence.[88]

There are interesting questions about this case. Unlike the case of Amoateng, who appeared to have solely embarked upon the act, never used the VVIP section even though he was a sitting member of the legislature at the time, and was never visited upon his arrest by any Ghana Embassy official in the United States, Amatefe's case was different. She used the VVIP section to board the plane. Upon her arrival and arrest at London's Heathrow airport, she was briefly visited by the Ghana High Commissioner in the UK, Mr. Victor Smith, according to reports. Thus, Amatefe's use of the VVIP section of KIA, her rapid admission of guilt, and her brief visitation by the top Ghana government official in the UK appear to suggest assistance from highly-placed political connections.

Furthermore, the speed with which the Narcotics Control Board (NACOB) attempted to release a joint statement that "Nayele [Amatefe]was arrested on the 10th of November, 2014 through the collaborative effort of the NACOB and its British partners,... and that they [British] knew she was heading to the UK," which was subsequently denied by the British High Commissioner in Ghana, Mr. Jon Benjamin, in a statement made on November 21, 2014, appear to suggest that the British High Commission had no knowledge here in Ghana about Nayele's activities. The British High Commissioner is reported to have stated that "any potential drug trafficker to the UK from Ghana is arrested here in Ghana and not permitted to board a flight in order to traffic drugs." In a subsequent interview, and probably calculated not to bruise diplomatic relationship and avoid any embarrassment to the government of Ghana, Mr. Benjamin attempted to clarify his earlier statement by noting that "we saw the need to correct what we thought was a factual inaccuracy but from our perspective, that doesn't in any way affect our determination to continue collaborating with NACOB, indeed the statement that you mentioned said that we have collaborated with NACOB for several years and we will continue to do that."[89]

---

88   "Nayele Amatefe to know fate today," (2015).
89   "What British High Commissioner said about Nayele's jail sentence," (2015).

In all these polemics and counter-polemics between NACOB and the British High Commission, one thing clearly emerges: Nayele's case appears to have elements of some kind of assistance from highly-placed political connections in Ghana. She was most reluctant to mention names, probably to avoid implicating and destroying the political career of somebody within the political hierarchy or she was possibly paid off to remain silent. Hopefully, such coincidences will not escape the notice of voters in Ghana, when the 2016 elections are held.

Subah Scandal

The Subah scandal involved an ICT company, that had a GH¢144 million contractual relationship with Ghana Revenue Authority (GRA) to provide it with telecommunication monitoring services in 2010. The full name of the company was Subah Info Ghana Limited and was a business owned by one Joseph Siaw Agyepong, also the owner of a waste disposal management company called ZoomLion. Probably, what is most interesting about Subah is that there were so many interlocking directorates. It also involved companies owned by the same person, Mr. Joseph Siaw Agyepong, with a number of both domestic and international affiliates. The report[90] revealed the following, among others:

1. Subah delivered no value for money, and in fact did not do any work at all for the people of Ghana to merit the average GH¢4 million it received monthly from the GRA.
2. The account records showed that Subah made several payments to a number of institutions and individuals, some of which are under the same management.

Sabotage Accusation against the Volta River Authority

It has been said that if you are in a hole, it is prudent to stop digging further. One of the fatal blunders committed by the NDC government is its inability to solve the electricity power crises, which has been collapsing several businesses in the country and causing job lay-offs. For example, the mining companies have been forced to lay-off close to half of its labor force and this number of employees is even higher with

---

[90] "Subah scandal is a clear case of 'create, loot and share' - Nana Akomea." (2014).

the medium scale industries[91]. This power outages problem has persisted for about three years under the NDC administration. This blunder has been made worse by the fact that high profile cases of corruption, which the government appears incapable of reining in, are rapidly alienating the sympathy of some voters toward the NDC government. And, as if adding insult to injury, this situation was not helped by a reported recent accusation of sabotage by the hydroelectric power generation company, Volta River Authority (VRA), by a government staffer, Mr. Sam George[92]. This accusation was made on the eve of a mass demonstration, dubbed, "Won Gbo," meaning "we are dying" of erratic power outages in the country. Rebuking Sam George publicly by a Deputy General Secretary of the NDC, Mr. Koku Anyidoho, that the president of Ghana did not support Sam George's accusation[93] only exacerbated matters for the NDC. For, if there was anything that came out loud and clear in this scenario, it was unmistakably a further proof that the NDC leadership is in utter state of confusion, and therefore should do Ghanaians a favor by gracefully bowing out of the scene.

Unbridled Borrowing

The heavy borrowings by the NDC government between 2009 to 2014, vis-à-vis, NPP borrowing between 2001 to 2008 in the equivalent of some $27 billion (i.e. the US dollar value of the debt at the time of borrowing) and some $ 5 billion (i.e. the US dollar value of the debt at the time of borrowing) respectively is resented by a significant number of voters, especially when there are no projects to show for those borrowings. Having gone through an international program that forgave a sizeable amount of its debt stock (i.e., Highly Indebted Poor Countries or HIPC) under the previous Kufuor administration, the NDC governments' insatiable and unbridled appetite for borrowing is certainly edging the country closer to the HIPC category again, which discerning voters are most reluctant to return to. These are likely to translate into voters penalizing the NDC at the elections in 2016.

---

[91]   "Gov't commentary on 'won gbo' demo 'insensitive' – NPP," (2015).

[92]   "Highly paid VRA engineers have questions to answer," (2015).

[93]   "Mahama is fed up with Sam George – Koku Anyidoho," (2015).

Another clear case of the seemingly endless and uncaring mismanagement of the economy is the recent borrowing of US$15 million from the World Bank, ostensibly to implement a Secondary Education Improvement Project in underserved high schools in Ghana.[94] It is a very unfortunate situation for Ghana presently, when a government that is unable to retrieve a wrongfully paid judgment debt of about US$30 million dollars still goes around on a borrowing spree with a further borrowing of US$15 from the World Bank. It is a clear manifestation of the politics of selfishness. This state of affairs is the equivalent of the aircraft of state being hijacked, with the captain having no control, and all citizens aboard held hostage up in the sky.

Ethnic Card in Election Campaigns

One behavior that is developing in election campaigns in Ghana that should be discouraged from gaining roots in our body polity is the playing of the ethnic card. While admitting it can be quite convenient and tempting for candidates, it is a dangerous practice that does great disservice to the unity and even the stability of the country, and should not be countenanced, whatsoever, by well meaning Ghanaians. Playing ethnic card is an election campaigning strategy where a candidate appeals to a particular ethnic group because he or she belongs to such a group, in hopes of exploiting or eliciting ethnic sympathy in order to gain political advantage and win votes. It can be done overtly or covertly, with the overt one being most dangerous. In all cases, it is divisive and is never in the best interest of Ghana.

After all, if one is seeking political office to serve the interest of diverse ethnic groups that comprise of Ghana, and not a particular ethnic group, it is only fair that one appeals to all voters in a non-discriminatory manner. In some ethnically and racially diverse jurisdictions of the world, such as the United States with relatively sophisticated and discerning voters, playing the ethnic or racial card may alienate voter sympathy and may even cause a candidate to lose votes. It is politically suicidal and a shot in the foot in such jurisdictions. For example, in the 1980 US presidential elections, the incumbent President Jimmy Carter had insinuated that

---

94   "Gov't secures $15m to improve secondary education," (2015).

the conservative Presidential Candidate Ronald Reagan was "racist."[95] Although, Mr. Carter quickly denied making such specific accusation, there were contextual implications to suggest that Mr. Carter meant exactly just that. Later, a high school student at a school where Carter visited during the campaign rebuked him of "soiling" himself with racist remarks. If you really come to think of it, playing the ethnic card is really a politics of immaturity whereby, a candidate who is incapable of convincing voters on issues and merits resort to the comfort and security of one's immediate own, like the little child who turns and runs to the mother whenever it is confronted with uncertain situation.

The NDC's then Presidential Candidate John Mahama played an overt ethnic card during one of his campaigns in 2012 in the North, where he appealed to Northerners to vote for one of their own and upgrade them from their traditional vice-presidential pairing slot.[96] However, it is hard to evaluate the impact of this style of campaigning on the outcome of that election because the NPP Supreme Court petition of 2012 in itself may have been a part of the conundrum of the outcome. Mr. John Mahama's indulgence in ethnic politics was hardly the first. In fact, his predecessor, late President Atta-Mills also played a similar overt ethnic card in 2008 presidential elections, with his famous "Adze wo fie a oye," [97] meaning it does not hurt to get someone from within one's own house or family to become president.

Recently, an attempt was made to scoop up "dirt" on the NPP through one of its leading members, Mr. Osafo Marfo. Using a leaked tape recording in which he is alleged to have remarked to some members of the NPP council of elders in the Eastern region that the majority of people in the country, from whose territories come 90 percent of the country's resources should control the political power and decision making.[98] In this particular case, Mr. Osafo Marfo cannot be accused of playing the ethnic card, even covertly. Although, Mr. Osafo Marfo has denied the recordings as being "doctored," assuming that the allegation is even taken at face value, Mr. Osafo Marfo was truthfully giving voice to an obvious fact about

---

[95]   "Jimmy Carter - Election of 1980." (2015).

[96]   "Mahama's dangerous ethnic tirades," (2012).

[97]   "Nana invades Mills' backyard," (2011).

[98]   "My alleged 'tribal' tape doctored – Osafo Marfo," (2015).

majority rule, which is the dominant factor worldwide regarding modern democracies in elections and referendum. He was stating an obvious fact that it was only fair that the majority group who also produce greater resources for the economic development of a country should have a greater political voice in decision making regarding the use of those resources. It is not anything different from public ownership of corporations where, the majority of common stockholders wield the power to appoint managers of the firm, and thus determine company policy. Having been running dry, the NDC campaign rivals and rented press are desperately looking for a juicy scoop on any leading member of the NPP. It is very ironic that the case of someone who makes unvarnished appeal to ethnicity for votes rather turns around to support an "invention" of tribal accusation against someone else.

One thing that unfortunately happens to public figures is that sometimes their statements can be deliberately taken out of context, if not concocted altogether, to achieve political expediency and score cheap points, especially in election times like these. To give an example of the hypocritical and propaganda penchant of the NDC government in this particular case, designed to score cheap political points, none other than the NDC Minister for Communications, Dr. Omane Boamah, is on record as suggesting that such statement spelled the doom of Mr. Osafo Marfo's political career.[99] The question that every objective thinker ought to ask is: "How could Dr. Omane Boamah fail to see the more damaging and divisive nature of the then Presidential Candidates John Mahama and late Atta-Mills campaign utterances which were rather quite direct and explicit appeals to their ethnic groups for votes?" And those candidates never refuted the media reports, implying they actually made those statements and accepted what they had stated.

Installation of Solar Street Lights as Quick Fix to "Dumsor"

Currently, the NDC government is trying very hard to install solar street lights across the country. As one travels down major roads, one finds few solar street lights dotted alongside these roads, particularly near

---

[99] "'Tribal comments' will destroy Osafo Marfo's political career – Omane Boamah," (2015).

entrances and center of some townships. Those are ornamental quick fix to serious and important problems that require permanent solutions and are only intended as political deceptions. Why now? They are attempts by the NDC government to present the semblance of showing to the non-discerning voter its commitment to ending "dumsor" or electricity load shedding exercise going on in the country. This is too little too late, and suggestive of a desperate attempt by a government that senses impending defeat and punishment from voters who have endured unprecedented corruption and hard times under the NDC's watch for far too long.

They are attempts aimed purposely at winning votes. The "dumsor" problem is rather hitting households and business places the most; not on the streets. Most importantly, electricity is needed in homes and business places. People need electricity to power their business equipments and their household appliances such as, TVs, radios, mobile phones, refrigerators, electric irons, computers, electric fans, room lights; and these items are not found on the streets. They are overwhelmingly found in homes and business places. Sooner or later, these solar street lights will give in to total darkness at the very places that they are now located, as they become defective through lack of spare parts and maintenance. We need to think in the long-term. They are only a scratch on the back of the intractable "dumsor" problem of the NDC. Probably, nothing is more offensive to discerning voters than desperate last minute attempts at solving long-neglected problems, through "I-don't-care-isms" and "yentie-obiara" or "we-won't-listen-to-nobody" attitude, only to appear to show commitment to the problem when it comes time for election, as if people cannot read between the lines.

NPP's Supreme Court Petition of 2012

Election 2016 is obviously not going to be an easy one, but the odds are very much in favor of the elephant party. A major reason why the odds favor the NPP in 2016 was the Supreme Court petition that challenged the election results of 2012. In and of itself, the petition was essentially a trial of the temperament, disposition, and character of the NPP candidate and flagbearer, Nana Akufo-Addo.

Prior to this trial, the NDC had succeeded in narrating and casting Nana Akufo-Addo as some kind of a hawkish, someone who was ready to set the country afire in pursuit of his political ambition of becoming president. They had successfully hijacked an exhortation speech by Nana to NPP sympathizers that he delivered at Koforidua in the Eastern Region during the run up to the 2012 election campaign. In the speech, Nana Akufo-Addo had stated that "the 2012 general election would be a do or die affair... after all, all die be die."[100] He made the statement to strengthen NPP polling agents and to challenge any unruly and intimidating behavior by NDC sympathizers, and also to be vigilant and not allow NDC supporters to steal ballot boxes, which had happened before. However, when Nana resorted to a peaceful approach to challenge the election results at the Supreme Court, this powerful NDC propaganda strategy came crumbling apart: the "violent" and "temperamental" Nana Akufo-Addo, who is hell bent on becoming president of Ghana even at the expense of inciting violence to achieve his goal, had admirably proved people wrong.

Nana Akufo-Addo's case is similar to the experience of ex-president Ronald Reagan of the United States, at least in terms of perceived temperament. A similar perception of "violent" and "temperamental" was crafted and cast on Mr. Ronald Reagan way back in 1981 when the Cold War between the two nuclear weapon superpowers, the United States and the Soviet Union, was raging. He was the "hot-tempered," 70-year old presidential candidate, ready to take the United States into arms race and ultimately bring the whole world into a nuclear catastrophe or the Armageddon. One report about a nuclear war was that the radioactive nuclear dust from an explosion will encircle the globe and invariably cause cancer in every country. The image was created that the more powerful bombs that Reagan was going to preside over "would be the greatest danger to the whole world," people thought. When the press gave him the opportunity to explain off that perception, Reagan said something to this effect:

> "I have lived through four wars at my age 70 years. War is not a good thing for any rational and responsible person to seek. But to sit down for the Soviet Union to manufacture more sophisticated weapons than ours, and turn around to take our

---

[100] "NDC press conference on Nana Addo 'All die be die' speech," (2011).

God-given freedom away from us and force us to live on our
knees for the rest of our lives, doesn't imply that as soon as
you elect me your president, I'm going to sound the war drum.
But we need to call the Space Defense Initiative by its proper
name rather than calling it Reagan's "Star Wars."

Ironically, he was to become the President who would break up the Soviet
Union Empire without firing a single shot, with his famous speech in
Brandengate near the Berlin Wall on June 12, 1987. "Mr. Gorbachev,
tear it down this wall," Mr. Reagan said, referring to the Berlin Wall
in Germany. That Wall was a symbol of Communist oppression, and
his speech was a challenge to Gorbachev's desire to increase freedom
in the Eastern Bloc through *glasnost* or transparency and *perestroika*
or restructuring. And it was torn down.[101] Today, Reagan is considered
among the best four presidents the United States has ever had in its over
two century's history as an independent state. Maybe, Nana Akufo-Addo
has been destined to lead Ghana, like Moses, out of this tyrannical rule of
unprecedented corruption and wanton dissipation of state resources that is
visiting untold hardships on Ghanaians. This was boldly stated by CPP's
Ivor Greenstreet at the NDC Congress in December 2014 at Kumasi.

Thus the issue of the age of Nana Akufo-Addo, given that there has been a
historical record in the person of Mr. Reagan who was sworn in as the 40th
president of the United States at 70 years, pales into insignificance. What
is important is that the person has a clean bill of health, truly committed,
and patriotic. That he is someone who is not just starting out with life
and seeing politics as a way of amassing wealth. But someone who has
successfully made out his life, and is primarily focused on developing the
socio-economic infrastructure of Ghana, probably for the reward of good
name, posterity, and immortality. That is, Ghanaians can say someday
with pride that we have, for example, a North-South high-speed railway
system or free SHS education because a Nana Akufo-Addo once lived as a
devoted citizen of Ghana. That Ghanaians can also repeat what American
late Roman Catholic Cardinal John O'Connor stated about Mr. Reagan
when he won a landslide victory as president in 1980 that, "there is a
mandate, which comes not from the ballot box; it comes from God," about
Nana Akufo-Addo.

---

[101] "Tear down this wall!," (1987).

Probably, nobody understood the import of the Supreme Court trial of Nana's temperament and character better than the NPP delegates at Tamale on August 13, 2014, who delivered a resounding victory for Nana to become the 2016 flagbearer and presidential candidate for the NPP. This conference was meant to prune down the number of flagbearer aspirants to five who would then go on to the second stage of the process to choose a presidential candidate for the NPP. Out of 740 ballots cast, Nana Akufo-Addo polled 598 votes, representing 80.78%. His closest contender Mr. Alan Kyerematen obtained a paltry tally of 59 votes, representing 7.98%. Mr. Addai Nimoh and Second Deputy Speaker of Parliament Mr. Joe Ghartey both obtained 22 votes each, which was 2.98% of total votes cast. Mr. Osei Ameyaw managed with 16 votes, representing 2.17% to pick up the last ticket to the October 18, 2014 national delegates' conference. Former Information Minister Mr. Stephen Asamoah Boateng who received 13 votes and former Trade Minister Dr. Kofi Konadu Apraku who pulled 10 votes dropped out of the race with 1.76% and 1.35% respectively.[102]

The second and final stage of choosing the 2016 flagbearer and presidential candidate for the NPP held on October18, 2014 was even more decisive. Out of the total number of votes cast by over 140,000 delegates in the 276 constituencies across the country, Nana Akufo-Addo won 117, 413 votes, representing 94.35%; followed by Mr. Alan Kyerematen who had 5,908, representing 4.75%; with Mr. Addai-Nimoh pulling 1,128, representing 0.91%.[103]

It is fair to suspect that the ruling NDC recognized this fact: that Nana Akufo-Addo's victory would torpedo the aspirations of the NDC in the 2016 elections. In other words, it spelt NDC's defeat in 2016. Therefore, the NDC, keenly aware of the principled nature of Nana Akufo-Addo, a win for Nana carried the likely implication of the application of the law of causing financial loss to the state to the hilt. This fact is something the NDC leadership was probably most fearful of, given the magnitude of corruption and fiscal indiscipline that has occurred under its watch. The NDC leadership's behavior appeared to leave no one in doubt

---

[102] "NPP Super Delegates' Conference: Akufo-Addo-80.78%, the rest-19.22%," 2014.

[103] "Nana Akufo-Addo Elected as NPP's Flag Bearer Again," 2014.

that Nana Akufo-Addo was their biggest headache, their gargantuan problem, and their unrestrained nightmare. Hence, they appeared to root for Mr. Alan Kyerematen for the NPP flagbearership. Even though, Mr. Alan Kyerematen eventually lost to Nana Akufo-Addo, the former has consolidated his position as the most formidable figure for the leadership and flagbearership of the elephant party next to Nana Akufo-Addo. Mr. Kyerematen resisted a lot of pressure from within the NPP to withdraw from the flagbearership race in favor of Nana. He must, however, be tremendously commended for the way he handled such pressure, by arguing rightly and convincingly that his whole idea of remaining in the race was not to make things difficult for Nana but to deepen democracy within the NPP and Ghana at large. In so doing, he more than succeeded in shifting the focus of the debate from his personal interest to a general commitment to democracy at large.

Transforming the Economy of Ghana: The North-South High-Speed Railway System

High-Speed trains travel at a minimum of about 250 kilometers per hour. At that rate of speed, a high-speed train travelling from Accra to say Bawku, a distance of some 800 kilometers, can do so in about three hours. I am quite convinced that by now, the NPP leadership has lined up several industrialization agenda for reviving the contract with Ghana. However, it must be noted that an important area that is pivotal for industrialization that has long been neglected is a North-South high-speed railway system to link the extreme parts of the North to the South of Ghana. What could so thoroughly demonstrate the ethnically sensitive and diverse character of the NPP than to embrace, as part of its agenda of developing the whole country, the construction of a North-South railway system? At once, it will become a monument of the NPP's commitment to the development of every piece of Ghana, with no ethnic region of Ghana left behind, as it will sweep across the length of the country. It is a very expensive project for a nation, but Ghana can learn from the experience of China, which is noted for undertaking this kind of project at one-third lower cost[104] than what it costs most countries. China usually does this with the assistance of the World Bank. Given the unprecedented scale of corruption and fiscal

---

[104] "Cost of High Speed Rail in China," (2014).

indiscipline that has characterized the NDC administration, it is very unlikely to secure any significant financing for such a project because investors generally do not have the confidence in the NDC government to undertake this kind of project. However, the NPP does enjoy investor confidence. Thus making free SHS education and construction of the North-South high-speed railway system are very likely to resonate quite well with the voters in election 2016.

Railway transport occupies a significant role in the transport system of a country because the development of trade, industry and commerce of a country is largely dependent on the development of railways. In fact, it is a national necessity, but it has long been held at bay probably because of the huge capital outlay that is involved. But where there is a will, commitment, and fiscal discipline; there is always a way. For example, it can be accomplished through project financing that involves public and private sources of finance, whereby the cost of the project is secured by the project assets and paid entirely from project cash flow, rather than from the general assets or creditworthiness of the project sponsors. It is also likely to attract a wider sponsorship because the landlocked northern SSA states, such as Burkina Faso may be interested, which could, in turn, sway the interest of leading international financial institutions. Its major drawback of inflexibility to individual requirements and costly intermediate loading or unloading operations pale into insignificance, vis-à-vis, the benefits such as:

1. Ease of congestions on our highways and minimization of road traffic accidents.
2. Encouragement of mobility of labor and thereby providing a great scope for employment, as the project itself will create employment avenues.
3. Speeding up decentralization in Ghana because people, cargo, and packages can move faster across the length and breadth of Ghana.
4. Facilitation of long distance travel and transport of bulky goods which are not easily transported through motor vehicles.
5. Quick and more regular form of transport because it helps in the transportation of goods with speed and certainty, especially in times of emergencies like famines and scarcity.

6. Help with the industrialization process of Ghana faster by easy transportation of raw-materials at a cheaper rate.
7. Safest form of transport and chances of accidents and breakdown of railways are minimal as compared to other modes of transport.
8. Carrying capacity of the railways is extremely large and elastic just by adding additional coaches; their charges are relatively cheaper due to its carrying capacity and will benefit the poor.
9. Intermediate loading or unloading operations can be largely taken up by the private transportation sector.

Hopefully, the future NPP government may consider this suggestion, as it attempts to revive the contract with Ghana.

CONCLUSION

"What's On Your Mind?"

At this stage, one may rightfully ask "what's on my mind?" Probably, the greatest and the most fatal mistake by the NDC government is its inability to recognize the age-old paradigm that "power corrupts, and absolute power corrupts absolutely." At the last NDC National Delegate Congress held on December20, 2014, at the Baba Yara Sports Stadium in Kumasi, it was reported that the wheelchair-bound CPP General Secretary, Mr. Ivor Greenstreet, made the following comments, "It was unacceptable that the NDC was meeting to elect new leaders, when it should have been meeting to re-evaluate its policies," which he said had plunged the country into an economic mess. Continuing further, Greenstreet said, "Currently nobody, I mean nobody is feeling your better Ghana. Continuous 'dumsor dumsor' [electricity power outages], corruption from top to bottom, left right inside out, and all the challenges you are facing are suffocating the Ghanaian people.... The most painful thing of all is that you don't care." In the midst of all those unprecedented corruption, the NDC, rather than seeing Greenstreet's admonition as an honest criticism or a nudge in the rib for the government to sit up, perceived him as an enemy.

In reply to Greenstreet, Mr. Sam George, an NDC communication member posted the following response on his Facebook page, "Ivor Greenstreet apparently needs some elevation to see the Better Ghana." George later apologized to Greenstreet as "a discourse about philosophy and thinking and nothing to do with disability."[105] But George's first response to Greenstreet's speech seemed to have had the full blessings of the president, who similarly made a quick response to the Greenstreet speech. President Mahama, who might have perceived Greenstreet's speech as scathing and daring verbal attack, referred to people who were not seeing the fruits of his policies as suffering from "selective myopia." By this

---

[105] "'Elevation' comment: Sam George renders apology to Greenstreet," (2014).

remark, the President meant that those who don't see the fruits of his good policies, which are bettering Ghana, are those people who have selectively chosen not to see them probably because they were not NDC members and see everything through political lenses. The president went further to say that it was not part of his responsibility to cure such people of their "selective myopia" or selective short-sightedness.[106]

The NDC leadership failed to observe a basic political tenet first published by Niccolò Machiavelli in 1513. Machiavelli warned politicians in *The Prince* to stay close to the people they are ruling. If the politician is "present, in person, he can discover disorders in the bud and prevent them from developing." Machiavelli further that if the politician "is at a distance in some remote part, they are [information] come to him only by hearsay and thus, when they are got to a head, are commonly incurable." If the politician is too "elevated" into the sky, the converse of what NDC Communication Team member, Mr. Sam George, told Mr. Greenstreet occurs: he fails to recognize the storm that will sweep his house away because his ears are in the sky and he can barely hear his people shouting. The president has probably stayed too long away from the people and he is being fed the "all is well" briefings from the sycophants around him. So the first complaint when he heard the people's voice through Mr. Greenstreet, it was probably news to him. As far as he was concerned and based on information fed to him by his handlers, everything was well with the people of Ghana.

Machiavelli further noted that the support of the masses is more important for the success of the politician. He urged the politician to renounce the praises of the sycophantic few around him who benefit from the politician's liberality, so as not to hurt the people who ultimately pay for the failures of the state. What makes the politician and political party hated above all is greedy or selfish behavior and "usurper of the property belonging to the subjects" or wanton dissipation of the national wealth and property of the people that retard the economic progress of the people and exact harsh economic sufferings. Machiavelli's centuries-old proposition is still applicable in modern political conversation, "men forget more quickly the death of their fathers than the loss of their property."[107]

---

[106]   Bokor, (2014).
[107]   Vergani, (1997).

I happen to subscribe to the idea that violence is not compatible with the nature of God and the nature of the soul, and that whoever would want to win and lead someone to his thinking requires the ability to speak convincingly and to reason properly, without threats of violence. I also hold that to convince a reasonable soul, one does not need a strong arm, or weapons of any kind, or any other means of threatening a person with death.[108] Towards the attainment of this objective, it is my utmost desire, and hopefully that of Ghanaians generally that we all want a peaceful election in 2016.

Two scenarios may, however, play out in the 2016 Election:

1. The NDC will lose the election and handover power peacefully like former President Kufuor did in 2008 to save the whole country from turmoil and to safeguard Ghana's role as the beacon and citadel of democracy in this sub-region of Africa.

2. The NPP will win, and the NDC will try to declare that they too have won, even though they know they have lost. The NPP may counter with the argument that the NDC could go to court. However, having experienced a Supreme Court outcome, the NPP will be most unlikely to go to court this time for any redress, and Nana Akufo-Addo may refuse to give a concession speech. The bone of contention will now be how the NDC leadership would be treated in the face of their unprecedented acts of corruption if they hand over power. They may be hesitant to relinquish power for fear of the application of the law of causing financial loss to the state. Since most violence breaks out at this stage, the country may be on tenterhooks. At this stage, the former Secretary–General of the United Nations Mr. Kofi Annan, Roman Catholic Church Cardinal Peter Appiah Turkson, former President John Kufuor, and former President John Rawlings may quickly convene an emergency closed-door meeting with the contending parties, namely, Nana Akufo-Addo and President John Mahama. At this meeting, they may try to forge a deal, especially with the application of the law of causing financial loss to the state. It may be similar to the case of a hostage taker who has committed murder, and asking the negotiator whether he will be sent to jail. "Sure, but the sentence could be reduced if you don't hurt any more people," the hostage negotiator might say to the hostage taker.

---

[108] "Full text of Benedict's XVI's speech in Germany," (2006).

REFERENCES

Acemoglu, D., Simon J., & Robinson, J. A. (2001). "The Colonial Origins of Comparative Development: An Empirical Investigation." *American Economic Review*, Vol. 91, 1369–1401.

Adeniran, R. O. (2014)."Dwarfs Cause Cedi Fall - Anita De Sooso." Retrieved on February 11, 2014 from, www.dailysguideghana.com/dwarfs-cause-cedi-fall-anita-de-sooso/

African Union Panel of the Wise. (2010). "Election-Related Disputes and Political Violence: Strengthening the Role of the African Union in Preventing, Managing, and Resolving Conflict," The African Union Series, New York: International Peace Institute. Retrieved on November 5, 2014 from, http://www.peaceau.org/uploads/au-electionviolence-epub.pdf

Alemazung, J. A. (2010). "Post-Colonial Colonialism: An Analysis of International Factors and Actors Marring African Socio-Economic and Political Development." *The Journal of Pan African Studies*, Vol. 3, Iss. 10.

Baker, P. (2014). "Crises Cascade and Converge, Testing Obama." Retrieved on January 15, 2015 from, http://www.nytimes.com/2014/07/23/world/crises-cascade-and-converge-testing-obama.html?_r=0

Bertocchi, G. & Canova, F. (2002). Did colonization matter for growth?: An empirical exploration into the historical causes of Africa's underdevelopment. *European Economic Review*, Vol. 46, Iss. 10: 1851

Blatberg, C. (2000). *From Pluralist to Patriotic Politics: Putting Practice First*, Oxford: Oxford University Press.

Bokor, M. (2014). "The CPP's Greenstreet hurts feelings but opens eyes." Retrieved on January 12, 2015 from, http://vibeghana.com/2014/12/22/the-cpps-greenstreet-hurts-feelings-but-opens-eyes/

Calhoun, C. (2004). Is it time to be postnational? ... Ethnicity, Nationalism and Minority Rights, (eds.) Stephen May, Tariq Modood and Judith Squires. Cambridge: Cambridge University Press.

"Cost of High Speed Rail in China One Third Lower than in Other Countries" (2014). Retrieved on 19th February, 2015 from, http://www.worldbank.org/en/news/press-release/2014/07/10/cost-of-high-speed-rail-in-china-one-third-lower-than-in-other-countries

"Full Details of Govt's $156 Million Loan Facility From World Bank." (2014). Retrieved on July 10, 2014 from, http://news1.ghananation.com/.../319157-full-details-of-govt%...

Cammack, P. (2006) "The politics of global competitiveness." Papers in the Politics of Global Competitiveness, Manchester: Manchester Metropolitan University.

Cammack, P. (2006). "UN imperialism: unleashing entrepreneurship in the developing world," in C Moores (ed.).

Chimanikire, D. P. (2007). "Brain drain of intellectuals and professionals from Africa: causes, issues and consequencies," *African Journal of Public Administration and Management*, Vol. 18, Iss. 1.

Clapham, C. (1985). *Third World Politics. Routledge.*

Cockcroft, L. (2009). "New universities could revert to polytechnic format." Retrieved on December 28, 2014 from, http://www.telegraph.co.uk/education/educationnews/4781291/New-universities-could-revert-to-polytechnic-format.html

"Compulsory education will make Ghana great, strong." (2015). Retrieved on January 12, 2015 from, http://www.ghanaweb.com/GhanaHomePage/NewsArchive/artikel.php?ID=342293

Dubbelman, B. (2012). "Political instability seen as threat to African economic growth." Retrieved on October 28, 2014 from, http://polity.org.za/article/political-instability-seen-as-threat-to-african-economic-growth-2012-01-19

Dumont, R. (1966). *False Start in Africa*. Worcester, London: Trinity Press

"ECG on the brink of collapse'– Power Minister." Retrieved on January 18, 2015 from, http://www.ghanaweb.com/GhanaHomePage/NewsArchive/artikel.php?ID=342957

Electoral Commission of Ghana. (2015). Retrieved on January 4, 2015 from, http://ec.gov.gh/page.php?page=484&section=50&typ=1

"'Elevation' comment: Sam George renders apology to Greenstreet." (2014). Retrieved on January 12, 2015 from, http://viasat1.com.gh/vone/news/local.php?postId=6340

Essert, M. (2015). "Obama just did for young people what no president before him has done." Retrieved on January 10, 2015 from, http://mic.com/articles/108060/obama-is-about-to-give-millions-of-young-americans-a-free-college-education

"'Even bad gov'ts contribute to nation building' – Mahama." Retrieved on January 29, 2015 from, http://www.ghanaweb.com/GhanaHomePage/NewsArchive/artikel.php?ID=343586

"Fitch Says Ghana's Massive Rate Hike Alone Unlikely To Support Cedi." (2014). Retrieved on January 10, 2015 from, http://www.rttnews.com/2265688/fitch-says-ghana-s-massive-rate-hike-alone-unlikely-to-support-cedi.aspx

"Four of Ghana's ruling elite charged with corruption" 2012, Retrieved on January 11, 2015 from, http://af.reuters.com/article/topNews/idAFJOE81601L20120207

"Full text of Benedict's XVI's speech in Germany." (2006). Retrieved on January 18, 2015 from, http://www.nbcnews.com/id/14848884/

ns/world_news-europe/t/full-text-benedict-xvis-speech-germany/#.
VLvLZck6nmY

Gadugah, N. (2014). "Don't we think? Lecturer charges at gov't's $3 million scandal." Retrieved on July 9, 2014 from http://www.myjoyonline. com/.../dont-we-think-lecturer-charges...

Gayton, L. & Bignold, W. (2009). *Global Issues and Comparative Education*, London: Learning Matters

"Ghana election: NPP considers challenge to John Mahama win." (2012). Retrieved on January 4, 2015 from, http://www.bbc.com/news/ world-africa-20671298

"Ghanaian general election, 2008." (2015). Retrieved on 11th Mrch, 2015 from, http://en.wikipedia.org/wiki/Ghanaian_general_election,_2008

"Ghana Election: John Mahama declared winner". (2012). Retrieved January 4, 2015 from, http://www.bbc.com/news/world-africa-20661599

"Ghanaian general election, 2012." (2012). Retrieved on January 4, 2015 from, http://en.wikipedia.org/wiki/Ghanaian_general_election,_2012

"Ghana extends voting to Saturday after technical hitch." (2012). Retrieved on January 4, 2015 from, http://www.reuters.com/article/2012/12/07/ ghana-election-idUSL5E8N71QL20121207

"Ghana On A 'Corruption Carousel.'" (2014). Retrieved on January 10, 2015 from, http://www.modernghana.com/news/566670/1/ghana-on-a-corruption-carouselasantehene.html

"Ghana Crude Oil Revenue 2011 – 2012". (2014). Retrieved on July 10, 2014 from, http://datablog.peacefmonline.com/pages/blog/15/

"GH¢144m GRA/Subah Scandal: Where the monies went." (2013). Retrieved on January 18, 2015 from, http://www.ghanaweb.com/GhanaHomePage/ NewsArchive/artikel.php?ID=289928&comment=0#com

Ghura, D. & Mercereau, B. (2004). "Political Instability and Growth: The Central African Republic." IMF working paper WP/04/80. Retrieved October 28, 2014 from http://www.sangonet.com/FichiersRessources2/CAR-polit-inst_wp0480.pdf)

Glaeser, E., La Porta, R., Lopez-de-Silanes, F., & Schleifer, A. (2004). "Do Institutions Cause Growth?" NBER Working Paper No. W10568.

"Gov't commentary on 'won gbo' demo 'insensitive' – NPP." (2015). Retrieved on 19th February, 2015 from, http://www.ghanaweb.com/GhanaHomePage/NewsArchive/artikel.php?ID=347315

"Gov't secures $15m to improve secondary education." (2015). Retrieved on 20th February, 2015 from, http://www.ghanaweb.com/GhanaHomePage/NewsArchive/artikel.php?ID=347380&comment=11399346#com

Hall, R. E., & Jones, C. I. (1999). "Why Do Some Countries Produce Much More Output per Worker than Others?" *Quarterly Journal of Economics*, Vol. 114, 83–116.

Hezel, F. X. (2014). "The Role of Culture in Economic Development." Retrieved on February 11, 2014 from, www.micsem.org/pubs/counselor/frames/culture_economic_developmentfr.htm

"Highly paid VRA engineers have questions to answer." Retrieved on 19th February, 2015 from, http://www.myjoyonline.com/news/2015/February-18th/highly-paid-vra-engineers-are-incompetent-sam-george.php

Hodgetts, R.M. & Luthans, F. (1994). *International Management* (2nd Ed.). New York: McGraw-Hill, Inc.

Hofstede, G. (1991). *Cultures and Organizations: Software of the Mind*. Berverly Hills, CA: Sage Publications.

Hofstede, G. & Hofstede, G. J. (2012) "Why is culture so important?" Retrieved on May 13, 2012 from, www.geerthofstede.nl

Ichino, A. & Giovanni, M. G. (1999). "Work Environment and Individual Background: Explaining Regional Shirking Differentials in a Large Italian Firm." NBERWorking Paper No. W7415.

"I won't allow my appointees embezzle state funds." (2014). Retrieved on January 9, 2015 from, http://www.ghanaweb.com/GhanaHomePage/NewsArchive/artikel.php?ID=339164

"Jimmy Carter - Election of 1980." (2015). Retrieved on February 22, 2015 from, http://www.presidentprofiles.com/Kennedy-Bush/Jimmy-Carter-Election-of-1980.html

Kunateh, M. A. (2013). "Ghana: Slash Ministers' Wages." Retrieved on January 18, 2015 from, http://allafrica.com/stories/201311090113.html

Kwettey, F. (2014). "Religious prayers useless for Ghana, Africa's transformation – Fifi Kwetey." Retrieved on March 19, 2014 from, http://www.ghanaweb.com/GhanaHomePage/NewsArchive/artikel.php?ID=303794

Lange, M. (2004). "British Colonial Legacies and Political Development." *World Development*, Vol. 32, Iss. 6: 905-922.

"Mahama's dangerous ethnic tirades." (2012). Retrieved on February 22, 2015 from, http://www.modernghana.com/news/430084/1/mahamas-dangerous-ethnic-tirades.html

"Mahama is fed up with Sam George – Koku Anyidoho." Retrieved on 20th February, 2015 from, http://www.ghanaweb.com/GhanaHomePage/NewsArchive/artikel.php?ID=347400&comment=11399480#com

"Management of economy requires discipline — Akufo-Addo." Retrieved on January 29, 2015 from, http://www.ghanaweb.com/GhanaHomePage/NewsArchive/artikel.php?ID=343708

Mensa, J. (2009). "Ghana: General election a lesson in democracy." Retrieved on January 4, 2015 rom, http://ghanaelections2008.blogspot.com/2009/04/ghana-general-election-lesson-in.html

Meredith, M. (2005). *The State of Africa: A History of Fifty Years of Independence*, London/New York: Free Press.

Mizuno, N. & Okazawa, R. (2009). "Colonial experience and postcolonial underdevelopment in Africa." *Public Choice*, Vol. 141, 405 - 419.

Musah, J. (2009). "Why NPP lost Election 2008." Retrieved on January 4, 2015 from, http://opinion.myjoyonline.com/pages/feature/200909/35529.php

Mwaura, N. (2005) *Kenya today: Breaking the yoke of colonialism in Africa*. USA: Algora Publishing.

"My alleged 'tribal' tape doctored – Osafo Marfo." (2015). Retrieved on February 22, 2015 from, http://www.rainbowradio.co.uk/2015/02/19/my-alleged-tribal-tape-doctored-osafo-marfo/

"Nana Akufo-Addo Elected as NPP's Flag Bearer Again." (2014). Retrieved on January 13, 2015 from, http://www.ghanacelebrities.com/2014/10/18/nana-akuffo-addo-elected-npps-flag-bearer/

"Nana invades Mills' backyard." (2011). Retrieved on February 22, 2015 from, http://thechronicle.com.gh/nana-invades-mills-backyard/

"Nayele Amatefe to know fate today." (2015). Retrieved on January 11, 2015 from, http://www.fillaweb.com.gh/news/general-news/nayele-amatefe-to-know-fate-today

Nkrumah, K. (1975). "Redefinition of Neo-Colonialism," *Readings in African Political Thought*, Mutiso, Gideon-Cyrus M. and S. W. Rohio, (eds.), 415-418. London: Heinemann.

"NDC govt practising 'Akonfem socialism' – Bawumia". (2013). Retrieved on January 28, 2015 from, http://www.ghanaweb.com/GhanaHomePage/NewsArchive/artikel.php?ID=291926

North, D. (1981). *Structure and Change in Economic History*. Norton.

"NPP Super Delegates' Conference: Akufo-Addo-80.78%, the rest-19.22%," 2014. Retrieved on January 13, 2015 from, http://www.myjoyonline.com/politics/2014/august-31st/npp-super-delegates-conference-akufo-addo-thrashes-six-others-in.php

Nugent, P. (2004) *Africa since Independence: A Comparative History*. New York: Palgrave Macmillan.

Nunn, N. (2007). "Historical legacies: A model linking Africa's past to its current underdevelopment." *Journal of Development Economics*, Vol. 83, Iss. 1, 157-175.

"Obama: US soldier's reported shooting rampage in Afghanistan 'tragic and shocking'." (2012). Retrieved on March 12, 2012 from 12http://news.yahoo.com/blogs/ticket/obama-us-soldier-reported-shooting-rampageafghanistan-tragic-190511568.html.

Odetoyinbo, D. (1994).*Why Is Africa Married to the IMF?* Retrieved on March 17, 2012 from, http://www.hartford-hwp.com/archives/30/031.html

Otabil, M. (2014). "Prayer not substitute for laziness." Retrieved on January 10, 2015 from, http://www.ghanaianreactoronline.com/news_details.php?newsid=12133

"Our partners ditched us in trying times – Mahama." (2014). Retrieved on January 15, 2015, from, http://www.ghanaweb.com/GhanaHomePage/NewsArchive/artikel.php?ID=317707

Owusu, W. Y. (2014). "Who leaked SADA's Unaudited Report?" Retrieved on January 11, 2015 from, http://www.spyghana.com/who-leaked-sadas-unadited-report/

Platteau, J.P. (2000). *Institutions, Social Norms, and Economic Development*. Academic Publishers & Routledge.

"President J. E. A. Mills orders EOCO to investigate Alfred Woyome's case." (2011). Retrieved on March 16, 2012 from, www.Ghanatoghana.com/ghanahomepage/president-j-e-a-mills-orders-eoco-to-investigate-alfredwoyome-case

"Rawlings angry at current state of affairs." (2015). Retrieved on January 5, 2015 from, http://www.ghanaweb.com/GhanaHomePage/NewsArchive/artikel.php?ID=341388

Rodney, W. (1972). *How Europe underdeveloped Africa*. Washington, DC: Howard University Press.

Sakyi, K. A. (2011). "Is Our Educational System in Ghana Globally Competitive?" Retrieved on October 24, 2013 from, www.ghanaweb.com/GhanaHomePage/NewsArchive/artikel.php?ID=228046&comment=7481111#com

Sedgwick, R. (Ed.). (2000). "Education in Ghana," *World Education News & Review*, Vol. 13, Iss. 2. Retrieved on October 24, 2013 from, www.wes.org/ewenr/00march/practical.htm

Shillington, K. (1989). *History of Africa*. Revised Edition. New York: St. Martin's Press.

"Subah scandal is a clear case of 'create, loot and share' - Nana Akomea." (2014). Retrieved on January 18, 2015 from, http://www.myjoyonline.com/politics/2014/May-19th/subah-scandal-is-a-clear-case-of-create-loot-and-share-nana-akomea.php

Tabellini, G. (2010). "Culture and institutions: Economic Development in the Regions of Europe." *Journal of the European Economic Association*, Vol. 8, Iss. 4, 677–716.

Taras, R. & Ganguly, R. (2002). *Understanding Ethnic Conflict* (2nd ed.). The International Dimension: Longman.

Tawfeeq, M., Smith-Spark, L. & Carter, C. J. (2014). "8 killed in Baghdad bombing as Iraqi PM declares amnesty for tribes." Retrieved on July 6, 2014 from, www.edition.cnn.com/2014/07/02/world/meast/iraq-clashes/index.html?hpt=imi_c2

"Tear down this wall!" (1987). Retrieved on January 13, 2015 from, http://en.wikipedia.org/wiki/Tear_down_this_wall!

Tettey-Enyo, A. N. (2009). "Why Ghana returned to three-year Senior High School." Retrieved on October, 24, 2013 from, www.modernghana.com/news/230835/1/why-ghana-returned-to-three-year-senior-high-schoo.html

"The Ethics Of 'Vickileaks'". (2013). Retrieved on 9th March, 2015 from, http://www.modernghana.com/news/503233/1/the-ethics-of-vickileaks.html

"The GYEEDA Report: Interactive Summary." (2014). Retrieved on January 11, 2015 from, http://datablog.peacefmonline.com/pages/blog/32/

Tischler, H. L. (1993). *Introduction to sociology* (4th ed.). New York: The Harcourt Press

Tonah, S. (2006). "The unending cycle of education reform in Ghana." Paper presented at the African Studies Association of Germany Conference, Goethe University, Frankfurt, Germany. Retrieved on October 24, 2013 from, www.rocare.org/jera/v1-n1/pdf/STEVE-TONAH-JERA-RARE-1.pdf

"Tribal comments" will destroy Osafo Marfo's political career – Omane Boamah." (2015). Retrieved on February 22, 2015 from, http://www.ghanaweb.com/GhanaHomePage/NewsArchive/artikel.php?ID=347567&comment=11404567#com

Troward, T. (2012). *Bible Mystery and Bible Meaning* (Classic Reprint). www.forgottenbooks.org. Originally published 1931.

Trompenaars, A. (1994). *Riding the waves of Culture: Understanding diversity in Global Business.* Burr Ridge, Ill: Irwin professional Pub.

UNDP. (2001). Human Development Report 2001. Oxford University Press: New York.

UNESCO Institute for Statistics. (2010). Retrieved on January 5, 2015 from http://www.uis.unesco.org/DataCentre/Pages/country-profile.aspx?code=2880&regioncode=40540&SPSLanguage=EN

"US embassy apologises to Ghana leader for tweet." (2014). Retrieved on January 19, 2015 from, http://timesofindia.indiatimes.com/ world/us/US-embassy-apologises-to-Ghana-leader-for-tweet/ articleshow/38813492.cms

Uy, A. O. O. (2009). "Can culture explain economic growth? A note on the issues regarding culture-growth studies." *Journal of Economics and Economic Education Research,* Vol.

Vergani, L. (Eds.). (1997). *The Prince.* Lincoln, NE: Cliffs Notes, Inc., p. 57

Weber, M. (1970). *The Protestant Ethic and the Spirit of Capitalism.* George Allen and Urwin.

"What are the causes of political instability in Africa?" (2014). Retrieved on October 28, 2014 from, http://www.answers.com/Q/ What_are_the_causes_of_political_instability_in_Africa).

"What British High Commissioner said about Nayele's jail sentence." (2015). Retrieved on January 11, 2015 from, http://www.fillaweb. com.gh/news/general-news/what-british-high-commissioner- said-about-nayeles-jail-sentence

Wikipedia, "Organisation for Economic Co-operation and Development." (2015). Retrieved on January 29, 2015 from, http://en.wikipedia.org/ wiki/Organisation_for_Economic_Co-operation_and_Development

Wikipedia, "Ghanaian general election 2012." (2015). Retrieved on January 11, 2015 from, http://en.wikipedia.org/wiki/Ghanaian_ general_election,_2012

Wikipedia, "Corruption in Ghana." (2015). Retrieved on January 11, 2015 from, http://en.wikipedia.org/wiki/Corruption_in_Ghana

World Bank. (2006). Africa Development Indicators 2006. Oxford University Press: Washington, DC.

ABOUT THE AUTHOR

Dr. Addo is a lecturer in finance and economics at the Catholic University College of Ghana at Fiapre, Sunyani. He was previously a lecturer at Mercy College in Dobbs Ferry, New York. He has made several publications; available worldwide, including barnes and noble.com and amazon.com

www.ingramcontent.com/pod-product-compliance
Lightning Source LLC
Chambersburg PA
CBHW050427290526
45786CB00003B/1429